"Carol's book cracks the closet community has all their ducks in a row. She writes with honesty, integrity, and grace of her life's journey with its struggles and triumphs while loving and trusting Jesus her Savior and Lord."

—**Jerry Skiles,**
Missionary, Shield of Faith Mission International

"Carol tells the real, raw truth of a woman's journey of faith through life and death, tragedy and triumph, setbacks and victories. She courageously shares the reality of the struggle that is called the walk of faith, overcoming, and transcendence, hoping to give comfort and encouragement to others who are too afraid to share their stories. Carol writes about beauty for ashes, the beauty of a redeemed and restored life found in the love of Christ, all to the glory of God. She shares her wisdom about what living a life of joy is all about."

—**Bryan Johnston,**
Pastor, North Bend Church of Christ, North Bend, Oregon

"Carol has beautifully and honestly told the story of God's faithfulness to her and her family through all the joys, stresses, and challenges they have faced. The book is filled with practical and helpful biblical principles that, if applied, will make anyone's journey through life pleasing to God and satisfying to them. I strongly encourage you to read Carol's book. I promise you will be encouraged and strengthened spiritually, as I have been."

—**Dennis Kizziar,**
Pastor, PebbleCreek Community Church, Goodyear, Arizona

"Don and Carol Bayne were very instrumental in our early years of walking with Jesus. They exemplified the life of Christ. They modeled how to trust in Christ when things were going well and when they were not going so well. They taught us how to study the word in such a way that it became a lifelong joy and habit for Kathy and me. Don Bayne was a lover of God, a lover of God's word, and a lover of people. That combination made him a wonderful pastor and mentor for many. Don loved the fact that Jesus could come back any day, and the animation with which he spoke of the return of Jesus produced excitement in those around him. If he were writing this paragraph, he would conclude it by asking you if you were ready for the return of the Lord Jesus Christ."

—**Gary and Kathy Chambers,**
Pastor and pastor's wife, Community Bible Church,
Lebanon, Oregon

# FROM PLOWING TO PREACHING

How God Redeemed and Used an Ordinary Farm Couple

Carol Bayne

LUCIDBOOKS

**From Plowing to Preaching**
How God Redeemed and Used an Ordinary Farm Couple

Copyright © 2018 by Carol Bayne

Published by Lucid Books in Houston, TX
www.LucidBooksPublishing.com

All rights reserved. No part of this publication may be reproduced, stored in a retrieval system, or transmitted in any form by any means, electronic, mechanical, photocopy, recording, or otherwise, without the prior permission of the publisher, except as provided for by USA copyright law.

ISBN-10: 1-63296-307-8
ISBN-13: 978-1-63296-307-9
eISBN-10: 1-63296-272-1
eISBN-13: 978-1-63296-272-0

Unless otherwise indicated, all Scripture quotations are taken from the New King James Version®. Copyright © 1982 by Thomas Nelson. Used by permission. All rights reserved.

Scripture quotations marked (TLB) are taken from The Living Bible copyright © 1971. Used by permission of Tyndale House Publishers, Inc., Carol Stream, Illinois 60188. All rights reserved.

Scripture quotations marked (NIV) are taken from the Holy Bible, New International Version®, NIV®. Copyright ©1973, 1978, 1984, 2011 by Biblica, Inc.™ Used by permission of Zondervan. All rights reserved worldwide. www.zondervan.com The "NIV" and "New International Version" are trademarks registered in the United States Patent and Trademark Office by Biblica, Inc.™

Scripture quotations marked (KJV) are taken from the King James Version (KJV): King James Version, public domain.

Special Sales: Most Lucid Books titles are available in special quantity discounts. Custom imprinting or excerpting can also be done to fit special needs. Contact Lucid Books at Info@LucidBooksPublishing.com.

*To Arthur Mueller, my husband of six years. His support, patience, and encouragement over the past three years have been truly amazing. He had no idea when we married at age 73 what would transpire as the Lord prompted me to complete the writing of God's involvement in the almost 50 years of my marriage to Don Bayne. Yet he has believed in me, championed my cause, and waited for my "retirement." He is an amazing blessing God has brought into my life in the lonely years of widowhood.*

*To Don Bayne, my husband of almost 50 years, in loving memory. He, too, encouraged me to be all I could be for the person of Jesus Christ. He believed in me when I struggled to believe in myself. Through loving me, supporting me in the time of our brokenness, and showing me the ways of gentleness and patience, he blazed the trail with me to healing, triumph, and victory.*

# Table of Contents

| | |
|---|---|
| Introduction | 1 |
| Chapter 1: God's Redemption | 5 |
| Chapter 2: My Early Years | 11 |
| Chapter 3: My High School Years | 17 |
| Chapter 4: Mr. Right | 21 |
| Chapter 5: Growing Faith | 29 |
| Chapter 6: God's Calling | 37 |
| Chapter 7: Prairie Bible Institute | 49 |
| Chapter 8: Miraculous Provision | 53 |
| Chapter 9: More Miraculous Financial Provision | 59 |
| Chapter 10: Pastoral Wisdom | 65 |
| Chapter 11: Raising Preachers' Kids | 69 |
| Chapter 12: Church Growth and Staff Difficulties | 75 |
| Chapter 13: Building Issues and Budget | 79 |
| Chapter 14: Equipping the Saints | 89 |
| Chapter 15: My Brokenness, My Story | 95 |
| Chapter 16: Help for Healing | 103 |
| Chapter 17: What I Have Learned | 109 |
| Chapter 18: Let's Learn from Job | 123 |
| Chapter 19: Do Not Give Up Your Dreams | 139 |
| Chapter 20: Finding Our Joy in the Lord | 149 |
| Chapter 21: Right Thinking about Joy | 155 |

| | |
|---|---|
| Chapter 22: Choices We Must Make | 159 |
| Chapter 23: Right Thinking about Pleasure | 173 |
| Chapter 24: Finding Joy and Beauty in Serving Others | 181 |
| Chapter 25: Fear of the Lord | 191 |
| Chapter 26: Beauty for Ashes | 195 |
| Chapter 27: An Eternal Perspective | 199 |
| Notes | 203 |

*The Spirit of the Lord G<small>OD</small> is upon Me
Because the L<small>ORD</small> has anointed Me
To preach good tidings to the poor;
He has sent Me to heal the brokenhearted,
To proclaim liberty to the captives,
And the opening of the prison to those who are bound;*

*To proclaim the acceptable year of the L<small>ORD</small>,
And the day of vengeance of our God;
To comfort all who mourn,*

*To console those who mourn in Zion,
To give them beauty for ashes,
The oil of joy for mourning,
The garment of praise for the spirit of heaviness;
That they may be called trees of righteousness,
The planting of the L<small>ORD</small>, that He may be glorified.*

—Isaiah 61:1–3

# Introduction

My husband Don Bayne and I ministered 33 years to one church, which grew in size from about 90 people to 700 by the time of his death in 2009. Donnie, as everyone called him, did not receive Christ until he was 26 years old. When he learned that Jesus is God and the Bible is truly the word of God, he made a total commitment to Jesus in every area of his life. From that point until the time of Don's death, God did what can only be described as a series of miracles, as He guided and provided for us time and time again. He led us to leave the farm (a huge step if you know farmers), sell our business, go to Bible school in Canada, and finally pastor the little home church where Donnie had found Christ as his Savior.

I am writing to my children, to all parents, and to anyone who might benefit from our story. A quick word to my grandkids—your grandpa Don is gone, and in not too many years, I will be gone, too. The Lord did extraordinary things in our lives, and if I do not record these remarkable episodes of God's involvement and leading, an accounting of God's amazing miracles will be lost. And to my kids—I want you to see what a godly man your father was. He was an ordinary man with an extraordinary commitment to an amazing God. We may not be leaving great financial riches, but I want the stories of the blessings of the Lord Jesus Christ on our lives to be our legacy and your inheritance.

Since the passing of this incredible man, I have felt the hand of God on me to record these miracles of leading, provision, and anointing. God is certainly glorified in the telling of such stories.

We love a good story, and we all have a story to tell. We are not the heroes of our stories, but we become the main characters because we are the ones who decide the direction our story will take. Most of our stories include times of brokenness, disappointment, betrayal, confusion, and shame. Certainly, that describes my story. We are all fallen, broken people living in a fallen, broken world desperately in need of a Savior and a hopeful ending. And that is what God gives us in Jesus.

My desire is to encourage all those who have experienced the pain of heartbreak, sin, and failure to find their hope and redemption in Jesus Christ. My story is addressed especially to parents whose hearts are shattered because of what has happened to their children. They need to know there is a hero—one who came into our world so He could enter our stories and provide meaning and a redemptive purpose to our brokenness and loss.

When God takes a person from the bondage of sin and corruption to victory and purpose, He receives great glory. However, I want to add that our stories need not include long trips to the far country of sin to be powerful testimonies of God's grace. My new husband, Arthur, determined as a young boy that he did not want to disappoint Jesus after hearing his mother tell stories of Israel's unbelief and God's disappointment with them. Yes, he needed the cleansing blood of Christ, but living a Christ-centered life from one's youth is an even greater testimony to the power and grace of Jesus than believing the lie that we need to experience the underbelly of sin to build a testimony.

On March 17, 2017, I believe the Lord led me to Isaiah 61:1–3:

*The Spirit of the* LORD GOD *is upon Me, because the* LORD *has anointed Me to preach good tidings to the poor; He has sent Me to heal the brokenhearted, to proclaim liberty to the captives . . . to comfort all who mourn . . . to give them beauty for ashes, the oil of joy for mourning, the garment of praise for the spirit of heaviness.*

Why?

*That they may be called trees of righteousness, the planting of the* LORD, *that He may be glorified.*

Ashes and mourning there will be, but Jesus came for our redemption, healing, joy, and victory.

I'm aware that this Scripture is a prophecy concerning Jesus. In the synagogue in Nazareth, He read this passage, sat down, and declared, *"Today this Scripture is fulfilled in your hearing"* (Luke 4:21). As His people, His church, I believe this commission and purpose is passed on to us.

If you know anything about track, you know the most precarious stage in a relay is the moment when one runner passes the baton to the next. If the baton is dropped, any hope of winning the race is basically over. So it is in the Christian race. It is the assignment of each generation to pass the faith along to the next. Israel failed more often than not in this task, and the next generation invariably wandered into idolatry, doing what was right in their own eyes. So it can be in the history of a Christian family.

Scripture instructs one generation to declare the mighty works of God to the next. *"One generation shall praise Your works to another, And shall declare Your mighty acts"* (Ps. 145:4). My heart's desire is to succeed in passing the baton to the next generation for the winning of the race and the declaring of the greatness of our God.

Psalm 34 was the first chapter of the Bible I ever memorized. The second verse says, *"My soul shall makes its boast in the* LORD; *the humble shall hear of it and be glad"* (emphasis added). How can one be humble and yet boast? That verse was a mystery to me until Christ revealed to me that boasting in the Lord and His promises is actually evidence of faith. We confuse this boasting with pride, and thinking we are being humble, we fail to claim and "boast in" the promises of our awesome God. This false humility does not please God and stunts our growth. Please know as I record the many incredible events in my life that it is in my amazing God that I make my boast.

My goal is to encourage, challenge, and motivate my descendants and others to live in such a way that God's glory and majesty are mirrored forth in the way we live and love. May He find His pleasure in us as we find our joy in Him.

# Chapter One
# God's Redemption

In the first five years of my marriage to Donnie, we went to church twice. Needless to say, my walk with the Lord was almost nonexistent. I knew the plan of salvation and could have led someone to Christ using all the correct Scriptures. But salvation is not a plan; it is not a prayer; it is a person—Jesus Christ. I had been trying to fill the void in my life with accomplishments—a college degree, marriage to a great guy, and beautiful kids. I tried parties, drinking, and what the world had to offer, but nothing satisfied.

It was March 1965. We had been married five years. Donald Lee III was almost four, Sherry (Cheryl Dean) was six months old, and I was pregnant with Bobbie Jo (Barbara Jo). Kimmie (Kimberly Sue) would come along 17 months after Bobbie Jo was born. After graduating from the University of Oregon in 1962, I taught English at Philomath High School for two years but was now at home, raising the kids.

I tried on several occasions to find my way back to God. I would pray, confess my sins, ask for forgiveness, and invite Jesus into my heart—again. I believed it was my faith that saved me. Isn't that what Ephesians 2:8 says? *"For by grace you have been saved through faith."* So I would try to be pious and make myself believe. Each time I tried, not wanting to be exposed as a fraud, I would not tell Donnie because he acted more like a Christian without Jesus than

I did with Jesus. Besides, what if it didn't stick? Also, I never managed to find a church. Each time I prayed the sinner's prayer, my focus on faith seemed to dissipate within a week or two. I would tell myself, "See? It didn't work."

This was all evidence of my lack of faith. Trying to convince myself that I had faith was not really faith at all. You can't look in the mirror and see if you have faith. So I stumbled on, getting farther and farther away from God.

One day while reading *Beyond Our Selves* by Catherine Marshall, I came to a chapter on the prayer of relinquishment. It spoke of the experience of having tried everything but finding that nothing had worked. That described where I was. I had tried everything but nothing had worked. I wasn't sure I even believed any of it anymore. Was there even a God? I still believed there was a creator God. Evolution didn't make any sense to me. But what did I believe about Jesus? I believed there was a historical Jesus, but was He alive, was He God, and could He hear my prayers, even the silent ones? I had a hard time imagining a God who hears the silent, in-our-head prayers we offer up.

I thought that maybe He existed and was who He claimed to be but just didn't want me. That was a distinct possibility. The way I had been living the past five years did not commend me to the heart of God. I had managed to stack up a pretty hefty mountain of sin—no use pretending otherwise.

Despite my doubts, I decided to try this prayer, this prayer of relinquishment, as she had called it. But it was with no emotion and with very little faith, if any. "Jesus, if you exist and can hear me and want me, you can have my life, such as it is, but I must confess, I really cannot claim to have any faith anymore." That was a pretty pathetic prayer, right? But that was it. That was where I was at that time.

I was expecting nothing. It was noon, time to fix lunch for Donnie so he could come in, eat, and go right back out to working on the farm. As I left that bedroom where I had been reading, I had an overwhelming sense of the presence of God. No bells, no whistles, no flashing lights. I cannot explain it, but I knew He had heard me. Something had happened. This time, I had come to Him with total honesty, acknowledging my helplessness and lack of faith. No more pretending to have faith. No more pretending about anything.

Immediately, I knew two things. They were indelibly impressed on my mind. *This time I must tell my husband, and I must find a church.*

Donnie came in for lunch, and I didn't know what to say. He ate his lunch and went back out to work, so I said nothing that whole day.

The prayer of relinquishment had worked so well, it was the only way I talked to God for days. I would simply raise my hands, declare my lack of faith, and cast myself on Him. *I don't know what to say, Lord, You will have to show me.* It was kind of cool. I didn't think of it as prayer. I was just talking to God.

For the next 24 hours, my faith would come and go. I would think to myself, *Carol, do you really believe all this—that there is a God who hears you and is present like this?* Each time the doubts and internal arguments came, I would again simply raise my hands and remind the Lord, *I told You I had no faith, God,* and the faith and His presence would flood me once again. I was learning to come to God just as I was. I think God must love it when we are totally honest with Him. He knows all about us, but we are often pretty clueless about ourselves.

And how was I going to find a vibrant, living church? I knew the church in our little community that we had attended one time was not what I was looking for. While standing at the kitchen window pondering this question, some unusual pink clouds stretched across the western sky. I remember telling myself, *What do you think God is going to do, just write it in the sky in pink? Ha! Let's not get melodramatic here, Carol.*

## From Plowing to Preaching

If God did not reveal where to go by Sunday, should I just dress the kids and myself and start driving? Would He direct me at that time? I remember chuckling to myself as I imagined God guiding the car and me. I had all kinds of cutesy visions of how God was going to direct me. I entertained myself with ideas and questions and was actually rather fascinated and curious of how God was going to do all this.

More churches were in Corvallis, 15 miles away. Perhaps I should head in that direction. These questions came and went for the next 24 hours. How would I know where to go to church? What am I to tell Donnie? *God, You will have to show me, but I told you I don't have any faith.*

Now, let me remind you that we had been married five years by this time and had attended church twice, each time at a different church. The next day at noon, just 24 hours after my prayer of relinquishment, Donnie said to me as we sat at the kitchen table for lunch, "You know that little church in Peoria? Off the main road there?"

"No, I never really noticed it."

"You have seen the sign in the little Peoria store about the church opening, haven't you?" he asked.

"No, I almost never stop there. Supplies are limited and prices are high. I just scoot on into Corvallis to shop."

"Well, anyway," he said, "the store owner and some community people want to get a church started, and they are going to have a service there Sunday for the first time. It has been closed 12 years, some windows are broken, and the roof leaks, but they are fixing it up. My grandparents used to go there, and I want us to go on Sunday."

Wow! It was like having God on the line speaking right to me. Amazing! You cannot even imagine the impact on my faith. There was the answer, loud and clear. Then I simply told my husband that

## God's Redemption

I had told God the day before that if He wanted my life, He could have it. I was not yet ready to make any big claims about being a Christian. Donnie just looked at me, said not a word, and went back out to work.

That Sunday, the kids and I went to Sunday school while Donnie finished milking. He was to come later for the preaching service. I shared with the few people sitting there in a circle what God had done in my life that very Wednesday. When I did, Roger, the American Sunday School Union missionary who was involved in opening the little church, had tears in his eyes. Tears also came to my eyes, and I knew this was home.

Our family began attending that little country church on a regular basis. We went there until we went off to Bible school, and when we returned, we would pastor that church for 33 years until Donnie's death in 2009.

## Chapter Two
## My Early Years

Very early on, I had two beliefs about myself, whether true or not. First, I was pretty smart. When I was little, Dad would come home with games or puzzles for me. I loved to figure them out without asking for the answers. I knew he was pleased because he would chuckle. There were questions like, "Why can't a woman living in the United States be buried in Canada?" "What gets wetter the more it dries?" "What do you find in the middle of nowhere?" "Bob's father has four children: Momo, Meme, and Mumu are three of them. Who is the fourth?" "Where can you find an ocean with no water?" I loved these trick questions. Sometimes I figured them out, sometimes not.

I don't think I was really smart, which was a rather rude awakening when I discovered that. Nevertheless, because of that, I never panicked on tests and always tested fairly high.

Second, I figured I was a thief. My uncle Dick was my favorite uncle. He told us stories and gave me lots of attention. He taught me to sing "Down by the Station, Early in the Morning" even before I could say the "r" in early. I hated my name because it had an "r" that I couldn't say for years—Carol (Cawo). I was the youngest of three cousins and younger than my brother. They teased me mercilessly with "cow" and "car," both of which I pronounced the same. "Do you mean "cow" or "cow"? In frustration I would say, "The one we are widing in," and they would hoot mercilessly.

Anyway, one day Uncle Dick came out to Oregon to visit us. He had to sleep in the living room, and as men often do, he placed all the change from his pockets on the end table next to the sofa. The temptation was too much for me. I don't remember if I took all or only some of it. But Uncle Dick knew. A million spankings would have been easier to take. Have you ever wished they would cut the lecture and just spank you? No, it just made Uncle Dick so sad. He was so grieved, so disappointed, and I was so ashamed. I had let him down, and now I was a thief. What could I say?

I am sure there were other reasons, but somehow I began to feel like I was building up quite a load of black marks. I was somewhat of a perfectionist even then. My room always had to be just so (even though the old ringer washing machine was stored in my room). Whenever I was cross or disappointed, it would show. Not pretty. My brother Bob was a gentle sweetheart, but I was more intense about everything and would stomp around, whine, or act ugly. So this load of black marks (better known as guilt) was piling up.

We lived in the housing projects in Lebanon, Oregon. Every week, a group of ladies from a little church in town came to the projects and held Child Evangelism classes at the housing project office. Sitting in a circle on the shiny hardwood floor, we listened to Bible stories. I can't remember much about those stories, but the little wordless book fascinated me. My heart was black with sin (the black page) until the Savior came in, and then His blood (the red page), I know, would wash me white as snow (the white page). And someday when I died, I would go and walk with Him on streets of gold (the shiny gold page). I didn't quite get it then, but that black page, indicating a black heart of sin, was a problem for this little girl.

About that same time, this same little church started sending a couple of men into the projects to pick us kids up and take us to Sunday school. They would walk around the row houses blowing a whistle, alerting us they were there. Fifteen minutes later, they would blow it again, and out we would troop, snotty noses, ratty hair, and all. They would load us into their car, and off we would go. This was back in the mid-1940s when parents were more trusting, and what parent didn't enjoy getting rid of their kids for a few hours on a Sunday morning?

Soon the church was holding revival meetings. Every night, this sweet couple came to our little church; we called them Brother and Sister Brazil. She would play the piano, they would sing, and then he would preach. It was then that I understood the wordless book. Jesus Christ had died on a cross and shed His blood (the red page) for me. But He had risen from the dead and was alive. If I would ask Him into my heart, He would come into me, and His blood would wash that black heart white as snow. That was good news! That's what the gospel means—good news.

When we were given the invitation to come forward to the little altar to ask Jesus into our hearts, I was there. That was almost 70 years ago, but I still remember my confidence that the load of sin had been lifted from me. Now I was washed white as snow. The gospel is so simple, even a child can understand it. In fact, the Bible tells us that if we don't become as little children, we cannot enter the kingdom of heaven. As we get older, I think we become too full of ourselves to humble ourselves to our need.

Then we were taken to the swimming hole and baptized. Baptism—what is that all about? Well, just as Jesus died (a very cruel and excruciating death, I might add), so in baptism I died with Him. I was buried with Him, and as He arose from the dead, so I arose from the dead, a new creation, my sins all washed away. The Spirit of Jesus had come into me and would help me live for Him. Baptism is a perfect picture of all this truth.

Does that mean I would never sin again? No. In fact 1 John 1:8 says, *"If we say that we have no sin, we deceive ourselves, and the truth is not in us."* But it goes on to say, *"If we confess our sins, He is faithful and just to forgive us our sins and to cleanse us from all unrighteousness"* (1 John 1:9). That is written to believers. I might add that this little muffin had to visit that concept on a regular basis. Mom was kind. She called me feisty instead of naughty. Whatever.

Does that mean we take sin lightly? No, it also says that John wrote these things so we won't sin. But if we do sin, *"we have an Advocate with the Father, Jesus Christ the righteous"* (1 John 2:1). What's an advocate? It's a lawyer. When we have a problem with breaking the law, we don't go straight to the judge. We pay a lawyer (often a lot of money, but not nearly the price Jesus paid for us), and he talks to (or advocates with) the judge for us.

Ephesians says that in Jesus and through the Holy Spirit we have access to father God. Wow! Awesome! Powerful stuff! Some people are very disrespectful of God. They might call Him "the man upstairs" or the "big kahuna in the sky" or use His name in vain. Not wise! Scripture says, *"The Lord will not hold him guiltless who takes His name in vain"* (Deut. 5:11). I told my brother Bob that one time, and he said he didn't mean anything by it when he cursed. I told him that was the point. "In vain" means to use in an empty, meaningless way.

By the way, when I learned that Jesus was always with me, do you know what I believed? I believed that Jesus was always with me. Profound, huh? One time, my two best friends who walked to school with me were mad at me. I was in sixth grade, and Mom had decided I should start wearing a bra. Oh, help! My friends were ticked that I was wearing a bra and they weren't, so they were mad and wouldn't walk with me. Prepubescent girls can be difficult sometimes.

I vividly remember reminding Jesus (and myself) that He was with me and I was not walking alone. That's a pretty cool truth for an 11-year-old to get hold of, don't you think? We are never alone and have no need to ever be afraid. That is what you call the fear of the Lord, knowing that God is always with us and aware of us.

## My Early Years

My two friends and I were soon buds again. (Too bad I would lose that fear of the Lord and forget about His presence at other times in my life.)

I loved vacation Bible school, although I could do without the crafts and was never impressed with artwork made of popsicle sticks and pipe cleaners. But my heart would burn within me when I heard the Bible stories. I was not a Daniel, who escaped the lion's den, or a David, who slew the giant, but their God was my God, and I was challenged to be like them. Pretty exciting! I would be fearless like Daniel; I would be a David after God's own heart.

I so longed to serve and please the Lord, to do great exploits for Him. While the moms were having meetings at church, some of us kids would play church. Someone would try to play the piano, someone else would be the song leader or pass the plate or pray, but I wanted to be the preacher. Our church had a woman pastor, and our larger sister church in Eugene, Oregon, had a woman pastor, Sister Perry, who was cute as a button. Their husbands were elders in their churches, and these women were under their authority, so I guess that made it okay for women to speak in the church.

The thought came into my head, *Maybe I should be a preacher.* But I remember immediately thinking, *No, I want to be a preacher's wife.* Hilarious! But, of course, you don't say that out loud to anyone. But I still remember those childhood thoughts. I married an unsaved farmer, but he eventually became a preacher. Now, isn't that interesting.

The love of my life was my big brother, Bob. He was one year ahead of me in school and was always my prince and protector. Together, we looked out for little brother Joe who was five years behind me. Joe, a sweet, delightful child, was saddled with the nickname "Honna," short for honey. How that stuck for years, I don't know. Poor kid! Later he cherished the name, especially after the passing of our precious older brother, Bob, in 2014. Bob always looked out for me, and in some ways, I looked out for him. My dad was away from home most of my growing-up years, but Bob was the man in my life that every girl needs.

We earned our money for school clothes by working in the berry and bean fields. If I worked extra hard and extra fast, I could buy the sweaters I needed to match the skirts Mom made for me. When I was still in elementary school, she let me stay home while she worked as a boss in the strawberry field. Picking strawberries was tough, and no one earned much, so she paid me five dollars per day to stay home and do all the housework.

I cleaned every room, scrubbing each wooden floor—soft wood with no nice finish—and having an occasional splinter to show for it. I also packed everybody's lunch. Mom left me money to shop for lunch things and for whatever I needed to have dinner ready when they came home tired after working in the fields. I wasn't much of a cook, but I learned to make spaghetti and a few simple meals.

Mom would help me take the old ringer washing machine and the rinse tub outside, and I would do all the family wash, hang the clothes on the line, and then iron whatever needed ironing. If I finished the chores in time, I would walk down to the community pool for a quick swim. Having Mom believe that I could do all that when I was so young was a huge boost to my confidence and sense of self-worth. Contributing to a significant need for the family was pretty heady stuff. I was determined to do better than merely a good job. I loved it. Of course, after the strawberries were done, it was back to picking raspberries and beans.

# Chapter Three
# My High School Years

My high school years were a hoot. I guess every high school girl wants to be popular. My mother told me to never pretend I liked anyone but to find something about each person I could genuinely like, and then I would not be a fake or a phony. I guess it worked because I was well liked by the other students and received many honors. My junior year I was elected prom queen, even though I did not dance (one of the many don'ts of my church).

The students elected me May Day Maid of Honor at the end of my senior year. What fun! I was never bothered that we were considered housing-project brats and from the wrong side of the millpond, so to speak. When girls were chosen for honors by the faculty, like the Lebanon Strawberry Festival court, I was never included, even though I was an honor student. All the princesses were daughters of store owners and business people in Lebanon. The rationale, I'm sure, was that they would help with the sale of tickets to determine who was queen.

My greatest delight was being elected to the cheerleading squad and elected head cheerleader my senior year. We called it "yell queen." Nice-sounding moniker—yell queen—but it fit me well. As head cheerleader, one of my jobs was to design the competition cheer for that year and teach it to the other girls on the squad and to the student body.

Bud Page, our principal, was very supportive and allowed me extra time at the pep assembly so the students would have the timing down perfectly. Timing and crowd control were a large part of the judging. We won the trophy for best cheer that year, thanks in large part to Bud Page.

Mr. Page would always ask me to say the opening prayer for the National School Assemblies, something that would never happen these days. I never knew how he learned I was a Christian. Yes, my high school years were a positive time in my life.

From the beginning of my sophomore year, I worked every day after school and all day Saturday at Britain's department store in Lebanon. No more bean fields. Yahoo! Mom worked cleaning house for Mrs. Britain, and that's how I got the job. I excelled at selling women's clothes, and I also managed the baby department upstairs. I started out at $0.75 per hour. Mr. Britain had no idea how well I could sell, and he decided once to put me on commission. That was the best check I ever earned. He immediately took me off commission.

In high school, my brother Bob and I would always check to see if the other one had lunch money or needed anything. He would occasionally tell me about some guy who wanted to date me. Then, more often than not, after a pause he would say, "Sis, you don't want to go out with him." That was all he had to say, and I wouldn't. He knew guys, and I didn't. He was my protector.

Dad and Mom probably would not have allowed me to date until I was 40, but they let me double-date with Bob. Mom told me that if I ever embarrassed him and he did not want to take me, he would not be required to do so. Years later, he used to joke that he made his spending money from boys who wanted to date me, but that was not true. It was definitely a joke. From as far back as sixth grade, I remember someone saying, "I can't believe you are brother and sister." I guess it was obvious that we were close, didn't fight, and looked out for each other. Did being poor contribute to that closeness?

I loved church youth camps, youth conferences, and church-camp meetings. I met some wonderful girls from Portland who took me in. Friendships were made there that I cherish to this day, friends like Zona Stevia, Bonnie Helfrick, Anita Mahack, the Timmons family, and others. I earned my stay at the adult-camp meetings by working in the kitchen serving tables and doing dishes. It was a great way to meet a lot of people. Most of the other kids I knew did the same thing, so we had a good time. It was sometimes a little messy but fun. One of the girls in our group was not allowed to work in the kitchen (her parents said their daughter did not have to work waiting tables). Of course, she was disappointed and missed out.

## Pacific Bible College

The a cappella choir from Pacific Bible College, now Warner Pacific University, would come to our church from time to time. It was a high point for me spiritually. The singing was incredible, and they would share testimonies about what God was doing in their lives. I would hang on their every word. That was my dream—to go to that college. I was committed and determined. I longed to know God more intimately. I knew from my freshman year in high school that my goal was to be a high school English teacher, but I wanted to go to PBC. I was hungry for God and thought I would find more of Him there.

I graduated from Lebanon High School on a Thursday in June 1957, moved to Portland on Saturday, started working in an insurance office in downtown Portland on Monday, and went to college at PBC that fall. I had gone to Portland earlier to secure the job. I lived with the pastor of a local church in Portland that summer. I had lived with them another summer when they pastored at the Lebanon church.

## From Plowing to Preaching

I went to Pacific Bible College for only one year. I would like to say it was a great experience for me, but in many ways it was not. I was disappointed. I think I expected the atmosphere to be more like what I experienced at youth camps or conferences. I was hungry for the refreshing times from the presence of the Lord I had experienced but did not know how to generate on my own. I transferred to Oregon State, but unfortunately, many of my credits did not transfer and I ultimately had to stretch four years into five to get my bachelor's degree.

While at PBC, I auditioned and made it into the a cappella choir. I was one of two freshmen who made it into the traveling choir, the main highlight of my time there. We traveled north for several weeks as far as Vancouver and Victoria, British Columbia. We would sing and give our testimonies, but somehow it all seemed flat. Where was the zeal? Where was the passion I thought I had seen when the choir came to our church?

I know my disappointment was more my fault than the school's. After all, this was not heaven. I knew I was not the most dedicated Christian, but somehow I thought I would find more spiritual life there. Where was it? They had plenty of rules—dos and don'ts—but there seemed to be a lack of love and passion for Jesus. *Maybe Christianity was only a religion after all*, I began to think to myself.

When I was preparing to move back to the PBC dorm for my second year, none of the guys who drove the school's pick-up were available to help me move. I couldn't use the bus to move, for crying out loud! So I figured the heck with them! I would go home to Lebanon and commute to Oregon State with my brother Bob. He would come and move me. I believe it was a God thing because it was at Oregon State where I met Don Bayne.

# Chapter Four
# Mr. Right

Donald Lee Bayne II was his full name, but everyone called him Donnie all his life. He was born on May 7, 1939, in Albany, Oregon, the first child and only son of Donald Lee Bayne and Mildred Frances Sanders of Halsey, Oregon. Although they were not Christians or a churchgoing family in those days, they were a very close and loving family. They worked long hours and didn't have a lot of money, but they were a fun-loving group. Donnie looked back on those years with fond memories.

My dad and his five brothers were not the greatest husbands, so when I was challenged at a very early age to pray about whom I would marry, I did just that. It's not hard to encourage young girls to pray about a future husband. Being told that God chooses the very best for those who leave the choice to Him made prayer sound good to me. I knew that left to myself, I would date and marry for all the wrong reasons—you know, somebody with swag, handsome, popular, the cool athletic type. As it happened, God gave me all that plus a quality person in Don Bayne II.

Donnie was an outstanding high school athlete in basketball, football, and track. He lettered in all three sports all four years and went to state in track his senior year, competing in the 220 and the 440. He had quite a scrapbook of articles by the time he graduated. Of course, since his sister, Sharon, was the high school newspaper

## From Plowing to Preaching

editor, there was always an article in the paper about Don Bayne. What a coincidence!

In the winter term of 1959, Donnie and I both hung out in the Memorial Union on the Oregon State campus where most commuters went between classes. But Donnie and I did not know each other yet. One day in March, my uncle Warren wanted me to take him to a swim meet on campus because Aunt Vila's younger brother was coming from Idaho to compete and then spend the weekend with them. Uncle Warnie, as we called him, said the meet was in the men's gym, which was right across the street from the Memorial Union building.

> God chooses the very best
> for those who leave
> the choice to Him.

Concerned that I might accidentally walk into a men's locker room, I asked a male student there to point out where we should enter to find the pool and the swim meet. He very sweetly put his arm around my shoulder, led me to the window, and pointed out the door we were to enter. That was my first encounter with this handsome hunk who was to become Mr. Right.

A few days later, I was antsy and thought I needed a break from classes. And I wanted to avoid this weird guy who was showing me some annoying and unwanted attention. Sally and Sally, two other commuters, were there at the Memorial Union with this same Mr. Right. They knew him better than I did and were both interested in him. When I suggested that the two Sallys, Mr. Right, and I skip class and go to the coast in his car that afternoon, they all concurred. We deserved a break. Yeah, right! Somehow I managed to ride shotgun while the other two girls sat in the back seat. By the time we drove home, Donnie and I both recognized a strong connection, and he was holding my hand.

It was a whirlwind courtship. It was March, just before finals, and we sometimes studied together. If dating him caused my grades to go down, I knew I would nip it in the bud. I do not think he cared much about grades. It was his sophomore year, and he was dropping out in the spring term for spring farming. He saw no point in a college degree when all he wanted to do was farm, and the farm was waiting and needed him. He always said he had gone to Oregon State to major in girls and football, which he did play his freshman year—football, that is.

## Horse and Rodeo Days

Donnie was a total charmer. One moonlit evening, he took me out to Granddad Bayne's farm to a fenced-in, ten-acre pasture near a wooded area. We stopped, got out of the car, and he gave a special whistle. Out of the woods came Flame, his beautiful Tennessee Walker/American Saddlebred mare. Without a saddle or bridle, he swung up on her, guided her around with his knees for a few minutes, and hopped off. Needless to say, I was duly impressed.

I did know a little about horses. In fact, I was preparing to try out for the Lebanon Round-Up Rodeo court primarily to please my dad. It was certainly not because I knew a lot about horses or was much of a rider. Actually, most horses other than my own scared me, but that is another story. In June, just a few days before the dance where I was crowned queen, Donnie proposed, and I was suddenly sporting a beautiful emerald-cut diamond on my ring finger.

I was nervous at the rodeo court tryouts primarily because he was there watching. He knew horses, was a great horseman, and knew I was not. Despite my nerves and to my surprise, I was selected queen.

As princesses and queen, our job was to go to the various rodeos around the state to represent and advertise the Lebanon Round-Up. If the location was close, we took our own horses. Sometimes, we flew to the more distant rodeo locations and then borrowed horses from some of the cowboys to ride out and advertise our rodeo. The two princesses who were true cowgirls always wanted to know if the horse could go fast, but I just wanted to know if he bucked or bit. Some cowgirl I was!

Another time, when we went tearing out on our horses, my horse made a quick turn, and I went flying off. Everyone gasped. When I got up unhurt, I made an exaggerated bow. What else could I do? Everyone was relieved, laughed, and clapped. Naturally, that all happened at the Lebanon rodeo in my hometown. Couldn't I have fallen off at some other rodeo? So embarrassing! My kids still love to tell that story. Why did I ever tell them? Whenever pictures of my rodeo days come up, they insist I tell that embarrassing story.

Yes, March to June, three months, and we were engaged. We were married the following March. I finished that school year and the next at Oregon State and then went to the University of Oregon my senior year, graduating with a bachelor's degree.

## Learning to Do Marriage

Donnie was such a kind, gentle husband, but he worked long, grueling hours. This was tough for both of us. We were married during spring break, and I was back in school at the end of that week. We lived in a tiny silver travel trailer under three oak trees there on the farm, where years later we would build our first new home.

That first summer, I worked with him 54 straight days bringing in the harvest on a little pull combine that had no cab. Every evening we came home covered in dust and grime from harvesting. But helping with a job so vital to the farm operation made me an essential element to the success of the business. Later, we got one of the newer combines with a cab over the steering wheel. But I was already becoming part of the family and part of the farm.

An eye-opening incident occurred one morning as Donnie was going out the door of our little trailer. I was complaining about some dumb thing. He paused, looked at me, and said, "Our marriage isn't going to make it, is it?" That comment stopped me in my tracks. What did he mean, our marriage wasn't going to make it? What I had said was no big deal. Didn't other families squabble like that? But then I realized that if it was not that big of a deal, why was I acting as if it were?

That incident had a huge impact on me and how we interacted. He was not accustomed to senseless arguing, and I did not like it, either. I needed to learn to discuss issues with more sense and less heat, not that I always managed to do that or that he always listened. But we were learning to do marriage more rationally.

One rule my dad had impressed on me related to responsible attention to the care of a car. If you ever hear a strange noise or knocking, you were not supposed to keep driving and make things worse. You stopped immediately and took care of the situation, or further damage would be your fault. You would be to blame.

So when our fairly new Massey Ferguson tractor had a major breakdown, I kept pushing to know whose fault it was. Finally, Donnie looked at me and said, "Stuff just happens." Hmm! It was no one's fault? There is no one to blame? "Not always," he said. Stuff just happens sometimes. That was an interesting but strange concept to me. I wanted someone to blame, someone to pin it on.

Blaming and faultfinding were pretty deeply entrenched in my dysfunctional thinking. Because of this indelible pounding into my head about cars, I extrapolated the same concept into other events. If anything went wrong, it had to be somebody's fault, right? Not always. *Stuff* happens. I had been rather adept at finding faults and flaws, especially in myself.

## Donnie's Early Training

It was on the farm that Donnie learned to work hard. His dad called him his "man-child." When he was just eight years old, he worked in the long, dusty harvest on the back of a combine, sewing the grain sacks as they did in those days. He was proud to know he could do a man's day's work. Close to the end of harvest when his granddad Leighton had finished the harvest at his place, he came to relieve the poor kid.

Donnie told me that had made him sad because he lost his job, and they must have thought he was not man enough. Today, they would call hard work like that child abuse, but hard work defined Donnie, and he loved it. What an incredible impact hard work can have on one's self-worth and self-confidence, especially when someone believes in them and their abilities at such a young age.

The summer before his freshman year in high school, his dad had a heart attack, and Donnie harvested the crop by himself. They lived in a close-knit community, and several farmers, knowing the situation, came at the end of the harvest and helped him finish up. Needless to say, Donnie was highly respected in the farm community for miles around. He knew how to work, and his work defined him.

> What an incredible impact hard work can have on one's self-worth and self-confidence.

That was before credit cards, but his dad put him on the family checking account when he was still in high school. Who does that? His dad trusted him and wanted him to have access to money if the need arose. He knew Donnie would never abuse the privilege.

These were events in his life that gave him the work ethic that made him so successful when he went to Bible school and then became a pastor. Farming 350 acres and managing and milking 100 grade A Holstein cows was demanding and punishing work. Donnie's dad commented later that his son had left the farm to go into the only work that was even harder and more demanding—pastoring.

For many years, I had prayed that God would guide me in choosing a mate. Primarily, he must be a good Christian. Donnie was not a Christian when I met him or when we married, yet I never had any doubts about marrying him.

To be honest, by this time, I had pretty much lost my faith. My walk with the Lord had evaporated, and I was no testimony to anyone. The first time I ever became intoxicated was when Donnie gave me some vodka his dad had at their house. It went down pretty smoothly with orange juice. But I became violently sick, and he put me to bed in his sister's room. That must have taught me a lesson because even though we did a lot of partying after we were married, I never really cared to drink much.

After Donnie became a Christian, he would occasionally say that the Lord had brought us together. In my mind I thought, *No, you were not a Christian, and God would never have led me to marry a non-Christian.* One day, I realized that had I been where I should have been with Jesus, I could no doubt have led Donnie to the Lord before we were married.

It was not God's leading that was faulty; it was my poor relationship with Him at that time. Some of my greatest regrets come from those years that I was not walking in faith and obedience. Yet God was faithful. Although Donnie was not a Christian, he was kind and good with more integrity than any man I had ever met. We were married on March 19, 1960.

## Chapter Five
## Growing Faith

Knowing that my faith was puny and also knowing the importance of faith, I kept looking inside myself and wondering how to evaluate and increase my faith. One day while reading the book *Twice Born Russian: An Autobiography* by Peter Dynamite, I came across a statement that basically said if you want to know how much faith you have, just ask yourself how much time you spend in prayer. He went on to say that many pastors and full-time Christian workers spend five minutes or less in prayer each day. I never finished the book and do not even know what became of it.

The idea was that if you believe (have faith) that God answers prayer, you will pray more. That made sense to me. I decided to keep track of how much time I prayed. I turned my little clock on the shelf so I could see it and got down on my knees and prayed. I asked everything I could think of, but the prayer still seemed pretty short. So I slowed down and prayed it all again before I looked at the clock. It was the longest prayer I could ever remember praying. Guess how many minutes it took. Five minutes.

*Okay, God, I don't know how to pray. You will have to teach me,* I thought. I decided I would get up 30 minutes before the kids usually woke up so I could spend at least 30 minutes praying. Since I already knew I could not talk to God that long, I decided to read the Bible as I began. I really did not know any good way to read the Bible, either, so I used my mother-in-law's big white family Bible and looked at the topics with special verses listed in the back.

As I read, I came across verses I remembered from my childhood. Overwhelmed with the faithfulness of God in continuing to pursue me and love me and woo me back to Him even though I had gone astray, I let my tears flow freely as the love of God flooded the banks of my puny little life.

> If you believe (have faith)
> that God answers prayer,
> you will pray more.

Our front door had five windows facing east that were always covered with precious little grimy handprints. As I looked out those windows, overcome with the love of Jesus and with tears flooding my eyes, I witnessed a glorious sunrise. Then sure enough, before long came the *tromp, tromp, tromp* of little feet coming down the stairs. It was morning, my time was up, and I had not even prayed.

I quickly ran through my list of prayer requests and purposed to do better the next day. That went on all summer. It was not until fall when I was returning to teach high school English at Central Linn High School that it dawned on me that I had asked God to teach me how to pray, and what I was doing *was* prayer.

That summer changed my life. God was speaking to me more than I was speaking to Him. Is that what prayer is supposed to be, a two-sided conversation with God? He certainly had more of substance to say to me than I had to say to Him. I returned to teaching and became involved in a high school Bible club, and God used me to influence kids and lead a number of them to a saving knowledge of Christ. The year before, they didn't even know I was a believer.

**Peoria Community Church**

Pastor and Mrs. Hayes from Eugene, Oregon, were older than 65 and retired but agreed to drive down from Eugene on Sundays to preach. They had a talented family of two sons and three daughters. Valeene, their oldest, was a missionary in Haiti and a very gifted musician. The two boys sang beautifully, as did Pastor Hayes. Because of their musical influence, our little church attracted musicians and singers, which gave the church a strong musical flavor.

Because Valeene was a missionary, the church was also quite missions minded. With this early influence, missions and music became an important part of our DNA as a church. Over the years, we attracted some incredible musicians and had some amazing special music events that truly fed my spirit. Pastor and Mrs. Hayes eventually moved into a home in the area. What a powerful inspiration they were to us personally and to what we became as a church.

Pastor Hayes would drive slowly down our dusty road from time to time and visit with me while Donnie was out working on the farm. He would ask me if Donnie was saved. I wasn't sure. I told him that Donnie was a good man, wanted to be in church, and believed the Bible was God's word, but I thought that if he were saved, he would tell me.

One time after Pastor Hayes's visit, Donnie asked, "How was Pastor Hayes? What did he have to say?" When I told him that Pastor Hayes wanted to know if I thought he was saved, he wanted to know what I said to that. I said, "I told him I didn't know but felt that if you were saved, you would tell me."

Donnie said, "Maybe I am keeping it a secret," and we both laughed. At that time I don't believe he even knew what it meant to be saved or born again. People often do not comprehend what salvation is all about. It is much more than attending church and believing the Bible is the word of God. Do they believe that Jesus died for their sins, rose again, and is alive? Have they recognized their need of a Savior, repented of their sins, surrendered their lives to Him as Lord, and been baptized? Donnie was learning, but he was not there yet.

Sometime later, we were planning to go to an Oregon State basketball game with three other couples—Al and Juanita Greig, Jerry and Diana Dyksterhaus, and Ray and Leah Robb. Assuming they would suggest we go to this well-known local bar after the game, Donnie and I discussed what we should do. It was interesting that Donnie had not yet received the Lord, but he was concerned about his testimony. We talked about it but didn't come up with a solution.

We did go to the game, and afterward Jerry suggested we go to his place. Great! We were off the hook, except when he said he had a partial bottle of Jim Beam, Al had some kind of booze, and Ray offered a six-pack of beer. We contributed a Beach Boys record, and we all went to the Dyksterhauses' house, drank, played music, and danced. Although I did not drink much, I did nurse a mixed drink all evening and made no stand for Jesus. Some testimony! (I had grown up believing that a committed Christian did not drink.)

## Donnie's Total Commitment

The next morning, Donnie said he was late with the milking and the kids and I should go on to church without him. No way. I was not going to be out late partying and then go to church, play the piano, and act like I was a good little Christian. I was a lot of things, but I was not a hypocrite. I was deeply disappointed in myself.

Donnie said, "You know what we can do, don't you?"
"What?"
"We can ask God to forgive us."

So we knelt down in our living room and asked God to forgive us. I believe that was the beginning of Donnie's salvation. When Pastor Hayes heard this, he suggested we make our profession of faith public. Romans 10:9–10 says we need to believe it in our hearts but also confess it with our mouths. There is no such thing as a secret believer. The Bible says, *"But whoever denies Me before men, him I will also deny before My Father who is in heaven"* (Matt. 10:33). Two weeks later, we went forward at that little church in Peoria, Oregon, to acknowledge our faith. And soon Don was baptized down at Hover's Pond.

Many, many times Donnie told people that it was a year later before his life really began to change. We were in a Bible study at the Hayeses' home, led by Mrs. Hayes. She showed us all the evidence of the resurrection of Jesus Christ and the truth that the Bible is the very word of God.

At the close of one study, she asked us all to pray a silent prayer. We cannot even remember what she asked us to pray, but in a silent prayer, Donnie gave everything to God—his farm, his business, everything. He also told the Lord that if he ever went away from this commitment, he wanted God to take everything from him. He would rather lose everything than lose this relationship with the Lord.

As we drove home that evening and he told me of his prayer. I said, "Wow, that would include me and the kids, wouldn't it?" For years he would relate how from that day forward his life was out of his hands and God was in control.

## Community Bible Study

Thus began a voracious hunger for the word in his life. Donnie had very little discretionary time, but the time he did have he spent reading the Bible. He was encouraged when he read about how even Abraham, the father of faith, failed. Surely, there was hope for him.

Isn't it amazing that someone else's failure encourages us? It shows that the heroes of the faith were human, too.

Eventually, we were able to double the size of the dairy herd and hire a man to help with the milking. Donnie had not grown up in the church and knew next to nothing about the Bible. Having a hired man allowed him more time to get into the word and the things of the Lord. These were some of the greatest times as we were growing up spiritually.

Wonderful, lifetime friendships were formed. The Greigs, the Doerflers, and the Robbs soon became very involved in our little church. The Bill Sim family moved to Peoria and bonded with us. Pat and Gary Keen, a newly married couple, moved to Halsey and began attending. Pat Keen, an incredible pianist, was a much-needed addition to our worship. She, Carlene Sim, and I formed a trio that became one of the delights of my life. Our little fellowship was growing.

Juanita Greig, Marianne Doerfler, and I became very close. Eventually, we each had four children, all within a similar age range, so whenever we got together we had quite a crowd—three women and 12 kids and sometimes three couples and 12 kids. We loved the Lord, and we loved each other. Our kids were all growing up together and forming lifelong friendships. And we were all growing spiritually.

One of our fun activities was playing volleyball as couples at the Halsey gym and going afterward to the Pioneer Villa for fellowship, french fries, and a coke. One evening when Dick and Linda Cooper were there, Linda and I were taking our turn sitting out for a game. As we sat and watched, Linda said, "You guys have something, and whatever it is I want it." Soon, she and Dick became believers, too. Just recently, Dick lost his battle with cancer. How good it was to know where he was going.

It was at that time that Psalm 37:4 grabbed my heart. *"Delight yourself also in the Lord, and He shall give you the desires of your heart."* I knew it meant that as I delighted in Him, He would put His desires in my heart as my desires, and then He could fulfill them. What an awesome verse. I had a deep longing to serve the Lord but was sure we would live there on the farm forever. Farmers' roots go very, very deep. So I gathered together any ladies in the community who were willing, and we would have Bible studies. I especially loved evangelistic Bible studies.

Donnie's desire to serve and know the Lord better was also growing, so we began having couples Bible studies. It was pretty much the blind leading the blind, but we treasured those times. We would persuade any couples in the neighborhood to come. Then we would read a passage and talk about it, always asking God to lead us. Poor Pastor Hayes probably didn't know what to do with us, but he just gave us his blessing, prayed, and turned us over to the Lord. He and Mrs. Hayes were quite past their retirement years by that time.

One time, it snowed heavily during our little Bible study, and Donnie had to hook up the tractor and pull everyone's car out one by one down our private lane and out to Peoria Road. Hilarious! How we laughed! We were making memories!

There is a passage in Psalm 18:32–35 that I have underlined in my Bible and put "Donnie" in the margin. It says, *"It is God who arms me with strength... Your gentleness has made me great."* You who remember Donnie best know that he was strong in spirit and character yet a very gentle, kind man. The church has often referred to him as a gentle German shepherd.

He would pastor one church for 33 years, but he never lost his servant spirit. He thought each person was special. He used to tell his people, "Nobody is big, nobody is little; we are all just medium." He could preach an inspiring and moving sermon one minute and the next minute be down on the floor with a spray can and rag cleaning up somebody's spilled coffee and think nothing of it. He simply wanted to keep the building God had provided clean and fresh for His people and visitors. If someone needed his attention, he would stop and attend to that person.

He was highly respected, but he was not full of himself. Early on, the Lord prompted me to pray daily that Donnie would be a man on whom the Spirit could rest without reservation. (I think God can't trust most of us with much of His power; we might blow ourselves up.)

Donnie never wanted to offend or annoy others. When we were still farming and had dairy cattle, he always worried about the cows getting out into a neighbor's fields. Of course, one day some heifers did get into a certain neighbor's nice green ryegrass field. They didn't do much damage, but the neighbor was irate. Donnie took the berating quietly, apologized, and tried to build stronger fences.

Later that same year when our crop was cut but not yet harvested, that same farmer was burning his field. The fire got out of control and burned up several acres of our crop. That meant lost income, not just trampled grass. When the fire was out, the neighbor was waiting for his scolding. He knew he had it coming. But Donnie only said, "These things happen." That was Don Bayne.

## Chapter Six
## God's Calling

One very rainy day in June 1972, something happened to Donnie as he was in the field chopping corn to feed the cows. He came to the door of the house, and it soon became obvious that he had lost his memory. He would say something, forget he had said it, and immediately repeat himself. He knew who I was, that he had four kids, didn't he? But who had plowed the north 40? Whose truck was that sitting in the driveway?

I called the doctor, and he said to bring him to the hospital. Dr. Knox, a neurologist, examined him and put him in intensive care. The doctor had me stick around because it can be very frightening to lose one's memory.

In spite of the seriousness of the situation, Dr. Knox and I found ourselves chuckling over Donnie's repeatedly asking if Dr. Knox was a relative of Marion Knox. One time Donnie said, "I asked that question before, didn't I?" When assured he'd asked it before, he said, "Well, are you?" He remembered he'd asked the question but still couldn't remember the answer.

Donnie was driving the nurses crazy, asking them the same questions over and over, so they called me to the intensive care unit. "Who was with the cows? Where was his dad? Why was he there?" Finally, a nurse wrote the questions with the answers on a piece of paper, put it in his hand, and kicked me out of intensive care. His memory came back at about 2:00 a.m. He thought he was just waking up with this sheet of paper in his hand, but he had never been asleep.

Dr. Knox could find nothing wrong with him. No fracture, no bump, but seemingly a very deep concussion. Lightning had crackled throughout the afternoon of pouring rain as sometimes happens in Oregon in June. We thought perhaps he had been struck by lightning while sitting on his very large-tired tractor.

Years later, an identical episode occurred while he was preaching, of all things. He was lost and just kept repeating himself and looking for his place in his notes. Quinton Hamel went to the pulpit to help this obviously distraught man. Donnie's shy secretary, Lisa Brown, who copied his notes, thought she had done something wrong and started to go up to help him. It was pathetic. Our doctor Glenn Petersen, a personal friend, was in the audience and recognized it as global amnesia, something he had recently encountered in another patient. He just walked up to the pulpit and led Donnie off the platform, down the aisle, and out to Donnie's office.

Everyone's heart went out to their dear pastor, and the service turned into an incredible prayer service. People prayed who had never prayed in public before. Of course, we realized what it was, took him home, and in a few hours, he was fine. We learned later that people rarely experience this a second time, but he had. At the time of the first incident, the neurologist had diagnosed it as a serious concussion.

The morning after that first incident on the farm, Donnie's mother visited him in the hospital and told him she thought he was working himself to death and needed to get out of farming. His response to her was "If I ever do anything else, I would go into Village Missions." That was a strange comment because it was American Sunday School Union missionaries who started our little church, not Village Missionaries. It was his first mention of a possible call to preach.

## God's Calling

When we left the hospital, the doctor said we should get away from the pressure of work, the farm, and the cows for a while. We called Cannon Beach Conference Center to see if there was a conference in session that we could attend. Mrs. MacNeil, the camp owner, said there wasn't a conference open to the general public because the Village Missionaries were there for their conference, but if we could find a place to stay in town, we could attend their meetings.

It was in Cannon Beach that Donnie told me what he had said to his mother—Village Missions, not the American Sunday School Union. And here they were at Cannon Beach. He could not remember ever hearing of Village Missions before. What a coincidence, right? This was the first of many coincidences in our journey toward a future of serving the Lord in full-time pastoral ministry. We have learned that there are no coincidences in the life of God's children. God had miraculously timed this little episode, getting us to a Village Missions conference in the middle of the summer when we normally would never have taken time away from the farm.

It was there in Cannon Beach in a little motel room that Donnie told me he knew I would think it strange, but he felt God was calling him to preach. I did think it was a little strange. I had no idea he was thinking anything like that. He was really rather quiet. Earlier, I had told him the testimony of a dentist who sold his practice to go into full-time ministry with Campus Crusade. After hearing that, he went out to change an irrigation pipe and thought it over. He told God that if He ever asked him to leave the farm to serve Him, he would obey. But, of course, he knew God would never call him to do such a thing—would He?

That was Donnie's approach to everything—if God asks me, I will obey. Earlier, he had been asked to give his testimony at a Valentine's banquet. He felt he had done a terrible job. Instead of saying, "Don't ever ask me to embarrass myself like that again," his response was, "I know I did a terrible job, but if God ever asks me again, I will do it."

Actually, he did not do a terrible job, and his testimony made a strong impact on John Miller, a man from the community who was there that evening. Donnie often suggested he was like the donkey whose owner hit him between the ears with a 2 x 4 whenever he wanted him to do something. When asked why he would do such a thing, the farmer explained that the donkey would obey any command; he just had to get its attention. The episode with the lost memory—global amnesia—must have been God's way of getting his attention.

So we went to the Village Missions conference. Donnie told Mr. Duff, the head of Village Missions, what he thought God was calling him to do. Mr. Duff suggested he would probably want to go to Bible school first. Oh, yes, his knowledge of the Bible was very weak, and he had a burning desire to know more. Mr. Duff mentioned Multnomah School of the Bible in Portland, which was close to us, and said there were several Bible schools in Canada. The only Canadian school he mentioned by name was Prairie Bible Institute in Three Hills, Alberta.

We met two couples at the conference, one from Multnomah and one from Prairie. We connected more with the couple from Prairie. And besides, the Canadian dollar exchange rate was much more favorable than the US dollar and might be better for a family of six. So we went home and wrote to Prairie Bible Institute.

Since it was well into July by this time and school started in August, Prairie suggested we continue to prepare and pray about it and consider coming the following year. Very wise counsel, and that is what we did. We needed more confirmation from God. Leaving the farm and selling the dairy business would be a significant and dramatic decision. And the following year, God did, indeed, totally confirm His calling for us to go to Bible school in Canada.

## God's Calling

One of the first confirmations occurred when Pastor Hayes decided to ask various families to take turns filling the evening service at church, and, of course, we were first. In fact, I don't believe any other family ever took a turn. That evening, the kids and I led some songs and sang a special number. Then Donnie shared with our little group what he thought God was calling him to do.

It was an amazing service. There was an unusual sense of God's presence. Without my knowing it, Donnie had made a deal with God. If this were, indeed, God's calling, He would enable him to communicate effectively what was on his heart. God had responded in spades.

Later, when he was asked to share again, he thought, "Hey, I can do this." That time he fell on his face, thus learning that previously it had been a God thing, a confirmation from God, but without God he could do nothing.

People in our small community were talking. "Have you heard what the Baynes are thinking about doing? What an incredible service the other night!" His parents, Don and Millie, were not saved at that time and were somewhat hurt when they heard what he had shared with others before confiding in them. But at that time, it was still only in the stage of being a possibility. Their salvation was one of our priority prayers, and they began to attend church with us.

In a service in which Donnie was leading the invitation song, he heard them whispering. His mother wanted to go forward, but his father did not. When she said she would not go unless he did, he went forward, not wanting to stop her. After they prayed, his mother was totally thrilled, but his father went straight to the car. He was thinking, "What have I done? How can I ever live the Christian life?"

In the weeks that followed, we could see Pa was struggling. He would often say, "All I ever wanted was for Donnie and me to work the farm together and make a decent living. What's so wrong about that?" Of course, nothing was wrong with that. Donnie began to waffle, thinking perhaps God was not calling us to Bible school. Maybe we were supposed to stay home, have Bible studies with his folks, and help them grow.

## Near-Death Choking

It was during this time that Donnie came in late one day to hurriedly eat some dinner before going back out to move the irrigation. All of a sudden, from the living room, the kids and I could hear him choking on his steak. He could not breathe and kept pointing to his throat. I ran to him and tried in all the wrong ways to help. When nothing worked, he ran out the door into the front yard. He did not want his little ones to see him die.

We were a mile from our nearest neighbor, even more from Pastor Hayes, and 15 miles from the hospital. If he passed out, what could I do? Then in desperation, realizing there was no other help, I finally cried out, "Oh, Jesus, help us!" When Donnie heard my cry, he said he felt a hand touch his throat and the meat was gone. He was okay.

As we all stood out in the yard holding each other up and looking around, we saw the irrigation going in the corn, the beautiful black and white Holstein cows, the barns, and the equipment, and we both realized none of that mattered. The only thing that mattered was our obedience to the Lord's call on our lives. That evening, the whole family went out together and changed the irrigation pipes, praising God for loving us and rescuing us. Prairie was back on the front burner.

Incidentally, it was the morning we drove down the road to Bible school that his dad, alone with God, agreed to quit fighting and totally surrender. He said, "Okay, God, You can have my son." That was the day he really began his walk with God. The one thing that had stood in the way was his unwillingness to give his son to God. What if we had not been willing to obey God's call to leave the farm? Would his dad have come to surrender, be saved, and grow? Our leaving was the very thing he needed.

As we began to communicate with his dad from Prairie, we noticed a remarkable change in his tone. When we came home at Christmastime, he told us of his encounter with God as he read Psalm 32 the day we left, and how he had released his son to God. What a changed man he had become. He could not stop sharing the Lord. In the short time he lived following this commitment, he influenced many people for Jesus. Later, when he and Donnie were ministering together—Donnie preaching and his dad leading singing—he shared that he and his son had never been so close, even though they were a thousand miles apart.

Donnie's dad passed away in January of Donnie's junior year at Prairie. He had suffered his second heart attack about five years earlier. At that time, Donnie had pleaded with God for his dad to live long enough to know the Lord. What if we had not been obedient? Again, *"Delight yourself also in the LORD, and He shall give you the desires of your heart"* (Ps. 37:4). What a Savior!

## More Confirmations

Dave Graffenberger, a missionary with Oriental Mission Society (OMS), heard about Donnie's calling to full-time ministry. He was so sure we should go to Haiti. Someone was donating a dozen heifers for the development of a dairy program to help financially support the Haitian believers and the mission program. A person who knew dairy farming was needed to run the program and teach the Haitians. Dave was sure Donnie was that man. He told us to write to headquarters and ask for a preliminary application.

Donnie struggled with this. He felt he could milk cows at home. He hungered to study the Bible, and he thought he was called to preach. Was that not God's calling? Finally, he surrendered to the Lord and told me to write OMS for the preliminary application.

If that was, indeed, what God wanted, he would obey. I wrote the letter and put it in the mailbox.

Our mailbox was about one mile from the house, and when I went back to the mailbox to pick up the incoming mail later that same day, there was a letter from OMS headquarters. "Thank you for your interest, but we have decided not to pursue that ministry. Continue with your plans for Bible school and contact us in four years."

Dave had been so sure about this that he had sent for the preliminary application himself. They were responding—with incredible timing. The very day our letter went out, their letter was delivered to our mailbox. That was another example of God's miraculous, "coincidental" timing. Again, surrender to Him was key. "Delight yourself also in the LORD, and He shall give you the desires of your heart. Commit your way to the LORD, trust also in Him, and He shall bring it to pass (Ps. 37:4–5). Here was another confirmation that we had heard the Lord correctly.

Loren Benson, a strong Christian, lived briefly in our community. He had a beautiful Romanian wife and a child but no house. He was actually living in a tent on property across from our fields. A diabetic, he was losing his eyesight. All of us younger Christians looked up to him as some kind of spiritual guru.

One day, he came to see us, and after a brief visit, he handed Donnie a check saying that God had told him to give it to us for Bible school or wherever the Lord was leading. Knowing his financial situation, we hated to take it. When he insisted it was God who had told him to do this, what could we say? When he left, we looked at the check and it was more than $80, which was a lot of money in the 1970s, especially coming from a family living in a tent. That was very humbling and lay heavily on our hearts, but it was a further confirmation of God's calling and His provision.

I might share at this point what I consider another one of those amazing coincidences that I see as God's leading and timing. Three years before this incident, I woke up in the night in a panic, realizing we had more than $3,000 in credit card debt. That was not entirely household debt. Much of it had come from bank transfers to pay feed and power bills for the dairy. Instead of overdrafting us, the bank would put $100 in our checking account and charge that amount on our credit card. Nevertheless, it was on the credit card now, and somehow I needed to get it paid. The next morning, I figured out a plan to pay it off in two years, which meant we could only spend what was absolutely necessary.

Our living room sofa had good bones, but the fabric was in shambles. A man in a neighboring community did quality furniture-reupholstering work. I called him, he came to the house, we picked out affordable fabric, and he took the sofa to re-cover it. After he left, I thought about my commitment to spend no unnecessary money. I called him, apologized, and explained my situation. Would he be willing to just keep the sofa, maybe re-cover it, and sell it to someone else? He graciously agreed and let me back out of our deal.

Now we had only two wooden rocking chairs for living room furniture, but I was staying on track to retire that credit card debt. About a week later, my parents came driving down our lane and into our carport. They had been to a furniture auction and purchased a sofa, loveseat, two lamp tables, lamps, and a coffee table. What a thrill to see God's provision! We took that furniture to Canada and then back to Oregon and used it for many years.

With sacrifice and determination, we paid off that credit card in three years. We made the last payment the month before we went off to Prairie Bible Institute. Had we had a big credit card debt, I do not see how we could have gone to Bible school. That urgent prompting had come three years earlier, two years before we had any idea of ever leaving the farm. But of course, God knew and had a plan. Amazing God! We have never since had a credit card balance that we could not pay within a month.

## God Assures Our Daughter

Donnie and I were not the only ones struggling with the need for confirmation of God's leading. The kids had their own issues. Sherry, our oldest daughter, was just going into second grade, and she loved the farm. She wondered why we were leaving. She was a little angry but knew we needed to be obedient to God's will and that if it were of Him, it would be okay.

She had heard the story of Gideon and the fleece of sheep's wool. When Gideon wanted to know God's leading, he asked God to make the fleece wet and the ground all around dry, which God did. The next day, Gideon asked God to do just the opposite, to make the ground wet and the fleece dry. Again, God did it and confirmed His calling.

So without telling us of her prayer, Sherry asked God to make one of the irrigation sprinklers blow out if He were truly asking us to leave the farm. Lines of irrigation pipe out in our cornfields held risers with sprinkler heads every 40 feet. The next morning, when she jumped up and ran to the window, one of the sprinkler heads had blown, and the water was spraying way up into the sky. God had spoken. *Okay, God, this must be Your will.* Isn't God good? He loves the little ones and wants their faith to grow and their hearts to be at peace.

## What to Do with the Farm and Dairy Business

At this point, we faced a major issue. What would we do with the milking herd? Dairy cows are milked twice a day, and you do not want to miss even one milking. Our idea was to either sell the whole operation or sell the cows and rent the land and milking parlor to someone who could later afford to buy the land. We had heard of young men wanting to get into dairying that way.

## God's Calling

Several potential buyers came from California and other places, but nothing seemed to work out. Many wanted to buy just the cows but did not want the milking parlor, the new cow barns, or the land. Dairy cows with quota were selling at a premium because that was one way an owner could get quota price for the milk, which was considerably more than surplus price. Cow buyers kept calling.

Finally, it seemed clear that God was saying to just sell the cows and quota. We could lease the ground to George VanLeeuwen and leave the barns alone. A motivated buyer contacted us. The price he was willing to pay was the highest we'd heard of then or for many years after. The lease money from George would make the yearly mortgage payment on the farm. That seemed to be the clear leading of the Lord. So we sold the cows and quota but not the land. We all had a strange feeling in our stomachs as the herd went down the road, truckload after truckload. Things were moving fast with no possibility of return.

Before Donnie could ever head out for Canada, he needed to know there would be a house in Three Hills where his family could live. The school knew of only one, a house owned by Alex and Bonnie Cunningham. But when we called, it had just been rented. To go to a place he had never seen, to a school about which he had only heard, and to a country where he had never been was one thing. But as a responsible father and husband, he would not take his family to Alberta, Canada, knowing the kind of winters we would face, without securing a house in which to live. That was a major issue.

One day later, we received a call from Bonnie Cunningham saying the little house was available after all. I remember her words as I became rather excited. "It is kind of like having God on the phone, isn't it?" she said. That seemed to be the final confirmation.

This all came together about a week before we needed to leave for Canada. We were accepted at the school. We had a buyer for the cows. George would lease and farm the land. But how could we transport our four young kids, our furniture, and our belongings to Three Hills, Alberta, Canada, some thousand miles away to go to school for four years?

Although not ideal, we thought that maybe one of our farmer friends' seed trucks would do. As we pondered this problem, John Miller, our nearest neighbor, called to say he wanted to rent a moving van for us. All these details were coming together quickly. Our heads were spinning. That week was a blur as we packed and made final arrangements. The afternoon before we were to leave, a group of men from the church were working like a bunch of bees, covering the silage pit with a tarp and weighing it down with tires. Inside, some friends and I were doing a little last-minute packing.

After selling the herd, we still had some outstanding debt at the bank. The evening before leaving and after the truck was packed, we stayed at Donnie's parents' house. Around their dining table, we stayed up past midnight with Mel Hanson, our banker, making final financial arrangements. He and his wife Linda would fly to Three Hills the next week to drive the rental van back home. Mel would arrange an auction for whatever farm equipment was left and apply that to the outstanding debt.

If you know anything about farm auctions, you know that very little cash is realized. Our auction was quite disappointing. Donnie signed an unsecured note for the remainder of the debt with the bank. Mel's superiors put a letter in his file questioning his wisdom as a banker. How was such a debt—more than $11,000—to be paid by a guy with a wife and four kids who was not even making any income but going to Bible school? It was not a wise banking decision. The bank was not the only ones wondering how this debt would be met. We wondered, too.

## Chapter Seven
## Prairie Bible Institute

Off we went to Bible school with a total of $1,500 to pay tuition for four kids and Donnie plus living expenses for a year. That year was tough for all of us, but finances were not the major issue for me. I missed the wonderful fellowship at Peoria. Before we left, I had sat in the little church sanctuary and cried like a baby thinking I was forever leaving everything near and dear to me, not realizing that in four years we would be back to pastor that very church.

As we traveled down the road with me driving our old Pontiac and Donnie driving the BeeHive moving van, I remember thinking, *What in the world have we done?* Donnie was so stressed that his mouth was full of canker sores. We had no idea what was ahead. We were driving in separate vehicles to a country we had never seen, and we could not even comfort each other. However, when I saw those majestic Rocky Mountains, I knew my God had created all that. He had clearly called, and He would take care of us.

Before we had even unpacked, Ken Penner, the principal of the high school there, was at my door asking if I would teach junior and senior high school English classes. Thinking this would help with our finances, I agreed, only to later learn that since we were there as students, I would receive what a student doing dishes in the cafeteria would be paid—$0.75 per hour. Big help! The plus was that we could shop in the staff store, and they would supply a babysitter for Kim since she would be in kindergarten for half the day.

Unfortunately, the school had no curriculum and no books or anything for teaching. It was a major struggle for me. Incredibly, we never ran out of funds to buy groceries or pay the rent and other expenses, and somehow, I made it through that year of teaching. We would occasionally hear of other student families who were down to nothing but potatoes. The finances we needed would come in from the church month by month.

One month, our car broke down, and a check came in for just what was needed for repairs plus tithe. My parents, Jack and Elouise Adkins, would send us a generous gift so we could make a decent Christmas for the kids. It was an enormous period of learning, especially for the kids, to trust God and see His faithfulness.

One funny incident that occurred had to do with my first pair of mukluks. They are beautiful, warm slipper-boots the Alaskan natives had taught my mom to make while my parents were living in Alaska. They looked more like boots than house slippers to me, so one day when there was a lot of fresh snow, I decided to wear them home from school. Home was across town about seven blocks.

Several blocks away from the school, I began to slip and fall every few steps on the icy roadway under the snow. The snow was soft enough, and nothing was hurt except my pride. I was between the police station and the Cunningham home and right near the town's skating rink. Each time I fell, I would look around to see who was watching. I had purchased a big fake fur coat at the Tillie shop, Prairie's version of a goodwill store, and I looked like a big brown bear down in the snow on all fours. I finally made it to where the ground was not so icy under the snow and was able to walk upright again. If anyone was watching, thankfully I never knew it. When I told my family, they thought it was hysterical—Mom down on all fours crawling home.

## When Willing to Obey, He Makes a Way

The college term was over in April, but high school did not end until late June. Donnie needed to return to Oregon immediately to work, but my principal requested that I stay behind and finish the school year. In spite of desperately wanting to go home with Donnie, I felt God would have me do the difficult thing. We decided the four kids and I should stay in Three Hills the extra seven weeks to finish the school year. Donnie flew home, and we were to drive home later.

Shortly after Donnie left, Ken Penner came to me and said I would have to go to immigration in Calgary to secure a work visa since I had been working on a student visa up to that point. The day after I returned from Calgary, Ken came to our home and told me immigration was not granting me a work visa, and if I continued teaching, there might be a problem getting back into Canada next year. We had come for Bible school, not for me to teach.

Wow! Another demonstration illustrating the truth of Psalm 37:4. *"Delight yourself also in the LORD, and He shall give you the desires of your heart."* Once I had been willing to obey, He made it clear I was free to go home to Oregon.

I packed up the old Pontiac station wagon with boxes precariously strapped high on top, looking like a scene from *The Grapes of Wrath*, and we headed home. Our guardian angel must have shaken his head and stayed close because we did make it the thousand miles. I remember having a terribly stiff neck, a backache, and a tension headache, but with a muscle relaxer I soon recovered.

## Chapter Eight
## Miraculous Provision

That summer, we all lived with Donnie's folks in the old farmhouse where we had lived before leaving for school. His mom was working as a cook at Oregon State, his dad was working at a mill in Eugene, and Donnie was working on Lewis Falk's farm.

We were making enough to live but very little toward school the next year. And how could we make a payment on that open note with the bank? Donnie figured that since we had always made the annual mortgage payment, maybe we could skip that a year and pay some on the outstanding open note with the rent money from George VanLeeuwen. We were saving as much as we could, but it certainly would not stretch to cover all these financial obligations.

In those days, farmers burned the straw left on the fields after harvest. That practice was becoming more and more unacceptable to those living in towns nearby. The farmers were quite skilled at choosing just the right conditions. They often burned at night when there was little or no wind and they could see the fires more clearly. They also kept water wagons close by for emergencies. Permits were required for every acre to be burned. The city of Eugene especially registered its unhappiness with the burning, claiming an unacceptable amount of smoke came into the atmosphere.

One day when the conditions were not at all good for burning and the governor of the state was in Eugene, burning permits were being granted throughout the entire valley. It did not take a rocket scientist to realize the farmers were being set up. Burning that morning would send an obscene amount of smoke into Eugene because the wind was blowing that direction. Farmers pretty much knew the burning would be totally banned after that day, so everyone who was granted a permit was burning. Entirely too many permits had been granted for any day, let alone such a windy day.

The wind was contrary, and fires were spreading chaotically and often beyond the farmers' ability to control them with their fire wagons. Every available fire truck from Salem in the north to Eugene in the south was out fighting fires. North of our farmhouse was our 40-acre piece that had been planted in wheat.

Harvested wheat stubble is never burned purposely like ryegrass because the fire is far too hot. Donnie's dad was home when he saw a neighbor's fire just north of our wheat field get out of control. He told me to get the kids in the car and get out of there because, with that wind, one very hot fire was headed our way. He watered down the north side of the house with a little water hose since our heating fuel tank was there, and then he and Donnie's mom left, too.

The kids and I went to a safe place on a road to the south where we could stop and watch. We could see flames higher than our two-story house billowing up from the wheat stubble. It appeared they were coming from the house itself. The kids, who thought their house was on fire, were all crying, "Our house is on fire! Our house is on fire!"

I said, "First of all, it is not our house; it is the Lord's. And second, if He wants to, He can save it. We just need to pray and give the situation to Him." So we all prayed a quick prayer with our eyes open so we could watch.

I said, "Look, kids, the fire is splitting." We could see flames shooting up above both sides of the house with blue sky between but none coming from the house itself. Donnie was five miles south fighting another fire when he saw smoke billowing up from the direction of our place. Halsey's fire chief was with Donnie at another location and assured Donnie that the fire at our home was under control. He was to remain and fight the fire at his current location.

When it was safe to return, we discovered the house had not been touched. The fire had scorched across the lawn in front of the house and across the garden in back. It had continued south and burned down the barns and new loafing shed, which were no longer being used. Talk about burning your barns (bridges) behind you! If Donnie had any idea of returning to dairying, it was pretty clear that option was no longer available.

The farmer whose fire had gotten out of control had a $25,000 insurance policy. Had we been renting out the barn and loafing shed for dairy use as we had originally planned, we would have been required to rebuild them. But since all the dairy facilities had been sitting unused, those funds were available to pay the open note and help finance the next three years of schooling. What an incredible answer to our financial dilemma! What a visible, faith-building event for our kids, for us, and for all who heard about it! All praise went to God.

Incidentally, the bank removed the negative letter from Mel Hanson's file, and he advanced in banking to have a long and prosperous career. Although financial issues are not the most important concern in the life of a Christian, they are often the most visible, and they often scream the loudest.

With the funds available, we returned to school the next year, and Donnie was able to intern under Pastor Hayes the following summer. The next summer, he was asked to help start a little church in Tangent, Oregon. He preached there Sunday mornings and at Peoria on Sunday evenings. He had been inspired by the preacher J. Sidlow Baxter to do expository preaching, and

Donnie taught through Hosea in his first sermon series. Those two summers of preaching were great experiences in preparing him for pastoring.

> Although financial issues are not the most important concern in the life of a Christian, they are often the most visible, and they often scream the loudest.

## God's Leading for Future Ministry

During Donnie's senior year at Prairie Bible Institute, we wrestled with the decision of where to go after graduation. We had learned that to discern God's will for such a major decision, three things needed to line up as one—the way lights in a harbor line up to direct ships safely in. Until then, it is not safe to proceed. The first light is circumstances or opportunity, and the second is the heart's desire. The third—and perhaps the most important—is what the Scripture says.

The opportunity was there. The church was asking us to come. The second was there. We did have the desire to return to our home area of Halsey and Peoria. But what did the Bible say? Many reminded Donnie of the word concerning Jesus in Nazareth. *"A prophet is not without honor except in his own country and in his own house"* (Matt. 13:57). Mrs. Hayes, who believed we should come to pastor the church, reminded Donnie he was neither a prophet nor the son of a prophet.

The missing piece came in a missions class at Prairie. Mr. Douglas, the missions teacher, told the class of the pattern in the early church.

## Miraculous Provision

God would raise up men from each local church to shepherd and lead that particular church. We were certainly from Peoria Community Church. All the lights had lined up. We had the necessary peace about returning to pastor our home church. The church took a vote, and we were called.

## Chapter Nine
## More Miraculous Financial Provision

We had seen my parents very little for a number of years and had planned to spend the summer between our junior and senior years with them in Fairbanks, Alaska. But when Donnie's dad passed away in January of our junior year, we knew we needed to spend that summer with his mom in Oregon. But for the following summer after graduation, we decided we should spend that summer in Fairbanks. We had good reasons to do so. My dad was even older than Donnie's dad, we had seen my parents only once in the last seven years, and we had questions about where my dad was with the Lord. And Dad was so sure Donnie could get some very good-paying work in Alaska. After four years of school, we were totally broke.

In our senior year at Prairie, two financial issues weighed heavily, especially on Donnie. One concerned having an adequate vehicle. The Pontiac station wagon had been on its last gasp for most of the time we were in school. We would often call it our wonder car because it just kept going. We really wondered, though, when it would break down for good.

Actually, it did break down several times on our way to and from Three Hills. One of those times, we had a lovely few days rest in Banff, Alberta, while the car was being repaired. Another time, it was a forced vacation in Kimberley, British Columbia, while we waited for parts to come in before the Pontiac could be fixed. The time in Kimberley gave us many opportunities to share Jesus, and several people did pray to receive Him as Savior and Lord. It was a very important time with our kids, all of us ministering together.

As we knelt around our bed in the motel to pray one evening, Bobbie Jo pointed out how many people we had spoken to about the Lord and how many had prayed. She had been keeping count. Many years later she reminded me of that experience. God is so gracious. He knew we needed that time as a family. If we didn't have the sense to realize it, He would just make the arrangements Himself. I know it was our concern about a lack of funds that often kept us from these times of vacation, but somehow the finances always worked out.

A second major issue on Donnie's heart, responsible man that he was, concerned housing for when we returned home. He knew very little was available in the Peoria and Halsey areas. At the dinner table one evening in our little house at Prairie, we took an empty milk carton, designated it as a house, laid hands on it and prayed, asking God for a solution to housing. Another time, the milk carton represented the car as we laid hands on it and prayed. At that time, all we could do was leave it in His hands, watch, and wait. Just recently, our daughter Bobbie Jo mentioned that she and her kids had done a similar thing.

So after Donnie's graduation in April, he went to Fairbanks to find work. The kids and I went to Halsey, where we would stay with his mom until grade school was out and then proceed to Fairbanks, too. Finding work was not easy, though. Almost a week into May, and Donnie still had not found work.

That day, Juanita Greig came down our long, dusty lane driving a lovely green Ford station wagon with that wood-paneling look down the sides, which was so popular back in the 1970s. I assumed Al had bought another car, a practice that really irritated Juanita. But she said, "No, this is your car." It took some time, but when she finally convinced me it was true, I was overwhelmed. A person had anonymously purchased it for us, and to remain anonymous, they had sent her to deliver it. To this day, we do not know who gave us that car.

My mom and Donnie had faithfully searched for work there in Fairbanks but had found nothing. Work on the pipeline was slowing down, and jobs did not seem to be available—not for him, anyway. Although he was discouraged, Donnie had felt God's assurance just that morning as he read Exodus, that as God provided for His children in the wilderness, so He would provide for us. When we called Donnie that evening and told him about the car, he was incredulous at first but then thrilled. When Bobbie Jo talked with him on the phone, she said, "And, Daddy, it even looks like you! You know, kind of like a governor." That was her interpretation of the wood paneling. We chuckle about that to this day. So there was the answer to one milk carton prayer—the car. God's answer to our need for a house was going to be equally remarkable.

When the school year was over in Halsey and the kids and I flew to Fairbanks, Donnie still didn't have a job. Everywhere he and Mom went, they said they needed a secretarial person. When I arrived, within two days I had several offers and began working at the University of Alaska.

That week Donnie got a job with a helicopter company, but the pay was only so-so, and there wasn't any overtime. My dad tried to get him in through the back door for one job, but Donnie felt it might require some dishonesty. He did not want to hurt Dad's feelings, but he knew if dishonesty were required, he could not accept the job. When the job did not materialize, he was relieved.

Soon after that, a great job opened up with a painting company at the pumping stations that offered amazing pay and lots of overtime. The job required blasting the insides of these huge steel tanks with steel grit and then retrieving the grit with huge shovels to reuse, all done in preparation for painting. Water is heavier than oil, so it would settle to the bottom of the tanks and rust the walls if they were not painted.

Donnie was a little soft after four years sitting at a desk studying. So the first few days just about killed him. The muscles in his back would contract and raise him right up off the bed when he tried to sleep. But you know Donnie. Nothing could stop him. He learned that by putting wet towels under his back, he could get a few hours of sleep. He worked 12 hours or more per day, seven days a week. A lesser man would have quit. Don Bayne knew how to work hard and hang in there when things got tough.

Fleur Alaska, the company building the pumping stations, wanted me to help manage their office. The senior man in the headquarters and contracts office was leaving, and they needed someone who could clean up the English and grammar in the letters and contracts for the man who would be left in charge. My writing and grammar skills were excellent. I had been teaching grammar and writing at the college for the last two years. The office job was a good one with 20 hours of overtime every week. But they needed someone who could commit to one full year. When they interviewed me, I told them I could not do that. We had told the church we would come in the fall. When my husband left to go back, I would leave with him.

When they discovered where he worked, they called me back and said they wanted me. I reminded them I could not be there for the year. "No problem," they said. They knew I would stay as long as my husband did.

What I didn't know was that this contract office was the one who hired the painting company, Lundeen Coatings, for whom Donnie worked. They assumed that with the unbelievable money Donnie was earning, he would never leave as long as they gave him work. When the job of painting the tanks was completed at all the pumping stations, the rest of the painting crew was terminated. He was given a job of random painting at all the pumping stations just to keep him working and to keep me at the office in town.

He would walk through one of the camps with a feather duster looking for rust he would then prime and paint. One of the guys watching him asked Donnie that if he got good enough with the feather duster, would they give him a real brush and some paint. Big joke! Not much painting was needed, but they were keeping him busy so I would stay in Fairbanks working in the contracts office.

During those five months, we were putting every penny in the bank. My mom and dad would not take a cent for keeping the kids and me. Donnie and Dad lived in the housing provided out on the pipeline. Because Donnie was making so much money each week, a large amount was taken out for taxes. Since we worked only those few months and had not earned much while in school the past four years, most of those taxes were eventually refunded.

Our employers could not believe we would leave jobs making that kind of money to go to a little country church in Peoria. But they did not know the Lord, and He was speaking louder than money. I had been honest with them from the beginning, so they had nothing to say when I announced we would be leaving in October and not the following June. We came home with a $21,000 cashier's check. That amount combined with our tax refund later enabled us to build a four-bedroom home on the farm property with a manageable mortgage. We came to understand why the Lord had allowed the cows to sell and not the land. It was the answer to the other milk carton prayer. These were very visible answers to prayer and great faith builders for us and our kids.

I might interject here that having a nice house was pretty much my god in my early days. During my growing-up years, my family had lived in some horrendous places, so having a nice home was a major motivation for getting me through college. The man I married could surely feed and house me. When I began teaching, I saved every penny I could to buy a house that was not an embarrassment for me and my kids.

My first teaching check was put into savings at the bank for that purpose. But I was immediately persuaded that it should go toward the purchase of a 40-acre piece of land north of our acreage, and the house could come later. Still, that goal had never left me. The call to Bible school and ministry came years later. Donnie was very much aware of my dream of a nice house.

During the process of our call to Bible school and ministry, Donnie said to me one day, "You know, if we do this, you will never have that nice house for which you have longed." I vividly remember weighing that in my mind for just a split second. But then I thought that God could have that dream. My desire to serve Jesus was greater than any house. Surely we would have some kind of roof over our heads. As it turned out, the home we built on the farm was far nicer than any house I had imagined when I gave the Lord my dream.

God is amazing. When we give Him our hearts and desires, He may very well give them back in abundance and better than we dreamed. I am now living in the third new home we have had built, each one more beautiful than anything I had ever envisioned, and all mortgage-free. And I have five rental dwellings to supplement my income now that Donnie is gone. God does seem to have a sense of humor. Trust Him! He loves to give good gifts to his children. He truly does know what is best.

> God is amazing. When we give Him our hearts and desires, He may very well give them back in abundance and better than we dreamed.

# Chapter Ten
## Pastoral Wisdom

While still at Prairie Bible School, I was terrified knowing we were being called back to our home church. I did not want to fail before friends with whom I had grown spiritually. I did not possess all the qualities I envisioned a pastor's wife should have—quiet, meek, pious looking, a piano player, and so on. I was none of those things. I saw myself as too outgoing, too assertive, and too talkative.

While still at Prairie, my dear husband gave me a book about being a pastor's wife. Page after page warned that if you could do anything else, you should not become a pastor's wife. He might be Mr. Wonderful, but she would do nothing right. She would dress either too classy or too frumpy. Her house would never be clean enough or homey enough. Her kids would never be perfect enough. On and on it went for more than 50 pages. When Donnie came home, I was fit to be tied. "Look at this. I will never make it." When I am scared, it comes out as anger.

He simply reached out, took the book out of my hands and said, "Okay, we will just not read this book." I never finished that book and never saw it again. It might have had some wise counsel, but I decided I would just go take a bath. While sitting there, I asked the Lord why I was so upset. Immediately I knew. It was fear, fear of failure.

When we had been home and pastoring for two months, the thing I feared most came upon me. A man criticized me for who I was and how I talked in his Sunday school class. I was devastated. I knew I could not succeed as a pastor's wife. What had I gotten myself into? It was on a Saturday evening, and for the next 24 hours, I was under attack. By Sunday evening, I was a mess.

Donnie finally said that if I was not supposed to be a pastor's wife, then he was not called to be a pastor. Immediately, I knew that was a lie from the enemy. I had no doubts about Donnie's calling. He was doing an incredible job. We prayed, and it was as though the lights literally came on and the darkness fled.

I asked Donnie why he was never criticized. He said that wasn't true; he was criticized sometimes, and he shared with me a criticism he had received. When I asked him how he handled it, his answer was very wise, and it has proved to be true to this day. He said he could not afford to let critical people derail him from what God had called him to do. That was it! Why would I allow the enemy to use a comment from an insecure, petty man to dissuade me from my calling?

That doesn't mean criticism doesn't hurt sometimes or that we ignore constructive criticism. We listen and learn and consider the source. Sometimes we may need to seek forgiveness, and sometimes we may need to change something. But from there, we must go on in the grace of the Lord. That was another important lesson for me. I try not to be easily offended. Most of the time, people do not even mean to offend me, and if they do, it doesn't do any good to waste my time and emotional energy worrying about it. Hurtful people are usually hurting people. I learned to extend grace.

## Financial Wisdom

Donnie never wanted to know anything about the giving at the church. He preferred preaching without fear of offending any of the big tithers. If the Bible said it, he would preach it. But he soon discovered that the church was in the red financially. Upon closer examination, he found that a $50 per month commitment to two missionaries had not been fulfilled. Finances had gotten tight, and they simply had not paid the missionaries.

So Donnie did some teaching with the elders and the board about the seriousness of broken vows, using especially Ecclesiastes 5:4–6.

*When you make a vow to God, do not delay to pay it; for He has no pleasure in fools. Pay what you have vowed—better not to vow than to vow and not pay. Do not let your mouth cause your flesh to sin, nor say before the messenger of God that it was an error. Why should God be angry at your excuse and destroy the work of your hands?*

When the seriousness of broken vows was explained, it was decided we would write these two missionaries, ask forgiveness, and agree to make up the deficit within one year, trusting the funds would become available within that time. God honored that decision, and the back commitments were paid in three months. The church finances were never again in the red for the 33 years Donnie pastored the church.

The Peoria Community Church congregation consisted of about 90 people when Donnie began as pastor. His first series of expository preaching covered Ephesians, and he took two years to preach through six chapters. Looking back, he marveled he had not bored the dear people, but they loved it.

He worked diligently on sermon preparation, believing it was an insult to his listeners to not come prepared. He started on Monday because some unforeseen demand could come up during the week and rob his preparation time. He was determined always to be prepared. He was not a Mondays-off minister. And every Sunday he rose at 5:00 a.m. and went down to the little church to pray and go over his sermon out loud.

## Chapter Eleven
## Raising Preachers' Kids

We knew that being raised as preachers' kids would be a stretch for our children. They had been very involved and aware of God's calling on our lives to leave the farm and go into ministry. Yet living under the pressure of being constantly scrutinized is not easy for any kid. We told them and reminded ourselves that our call to be parents preceded our call to pastoral ministry.

We diligently endeavored to instill in our children a sense of self-worth and value. As each of our daughters approached dating age, Donnie would announce that he was going to take her on a one-on-one father-daughter date. As the day of their date approached, each one was a little nervous. What was Dad going to talk about? Would it be embarrassing?

On the date, they discussed goals such as purity before marriage, appropriate behavior with a boy, and to never talk about marriage on a date. If a boy ever brought up marriage, she was to instruct him he was not to talk about that with her. He needed to talk with Dad first. Of course, that would nip it in the bud. Donnie knew that discussion of "I want to marry you" implies inappropriate intimacy.

Kids have a tendency to think it's nobody's business but their own about whom they eventually marry. So Donnie made a chart that depicted several generations, to the third and fourth generations, showing how many people would be affected by their eventual marriage. It was important stuff for them to understand.

At this point, Donnie asked each daughter if she would agree to tell any guy who wanted a date with her that he would need to talk to her father first and get his permission. This was sure to screen out young men with wrong motives. You might think this was a damper on prospective dates. But just the opposite was true. They were lovely girls, and guys lined up to date them.

Donnie's talk with the young men became more and more direct as each one got older. He wanted each daughter and any prospective boyfriend to realize that she was highly valued, of great worth, and a real treasure. You don't mess with God's property. Donnie even explained that although he would not be present on their dates, God would be there. Were they to violate his daughter's standards and goals, his prayer was that lightning would strike them. Ha! That, of course, became a source of humor at the Christian school they attended. One boy jested about looking cautiously around for lightning to strike.

We chuckle, of course, but protecting our children is important business. Raising kids, especially girls, during the dating years can be pretty dicey. The decisions and choices made during these formative years will follow them through life.

## Evangelism

God used Donnie and me so many times to bring people to a saving knowledge of Jesus. What a privileged couple we have been. So many lives touched and so many more stories I could tell. And so many people going on and serving the Lord. What an exciting and meaningful life! And to think that at one time I was afraid the Christian life might be boring. Being yoked with the Lord of the universe is an exciting, meaningful adventure. When you ask God to author your life, there are no monotonous chapters.

One person who came to Jesus was Cliff Bass, a man about the same age as Donnie's parents. Cliff had known Donnie since Donnie was a kid. He had Christian parents, but he was not a believer. He had been divorced for many years, lived alone, and was quite a "rounder," sometimes even buying alcohol for underage kids in the community. One day, his daughter came to Donnie and said her dad was in the hospital with a brain aneurysm and might not live, and would Donnie go see him. When Donnie went immediately and shared the gospel with him, he found Cliff's problem was that he did not believe he could live the Christian life. What would happen when he sinned?

> Being yoked with the Lord of the universe is an exciting, meaningful adventure.

Donnie explained to him that 1 John was written to believers, and it says, *"If we say that we have no sin, we deceive ourselves, and the truth is not in us. If we confess our sins, He is faithful and just to forgive us our sins and to cleanse us from all unrighteousness"* (1 John 1:8–9). No one lives totally without sin, but Jesus is our advocate with the Father for those times we do sin. What we need to do is confess and restore fellowship with Him. His blood cleanses us.

When Cliff heard this, his comment was, "I never heard it like this before." But he wanted his 80-year-old father to be there when he prayed. So he asked if Donnie would go get him.

Donnie went immediately to get Mr. Bass. When they returned to the hospital, Cliff said, "I thought you would never get back." Together they prayed. Cliff acknowledged he was a sinner and asked

Jesus to forgive him and change him into the man God wanted him to be. He did survive and got out of the hospital. What a changed man! All he could think of was sharing Jesus with his old drinking buddies. Many times, he would call Donnie and tell him they had to go talk to someone. He was in a wheelchair and carried a towel around his neck to wipe his face because he was so easily moved to tears.

One time, Cliff called to say they had to go to the hospital to see a man who was on his deathbed. Many years before, this man had come between Cliff and his wife, Eunice, the love of Cliff's life. Cliff never remarried after their divorce. You would think he would have bitterness toward the man, but his concern was for this man's lost condition and that he would go to hell. After Cliff shared the gospel, the man's response was, "I have been too wicked; God could never forgive me."

Cliff said, "If God can forgive my sins, He can forgive yours." Agreeing with that, the man prayed, asked forgiveness for his sins, and received Christ as his Savior. Donnie tried to teach Cliff that he could lead these men to Jesus without him, but Cliff always insisted that Donnie go with him to explain the gospel.

On another occasion, they went to the hospital to see another older man, and when they shared the gospel, the guy prayed to receive Christ. A few days later, Donnie was in the hospital to see someone else, and this same man was sitting in a wheelchair in the hall. Donnie tried to converse with him and could see the man did not hear or understand a word he said. Just then the guy's son-in-law came up, and Donnie explained how he and Cliff had been in earlier, and the man had understood and prayed to receive Christ. Now he did not seem to hear anything.

The son-in-law said, "Yes, Dad is stone-deaf." But he also knew that his father-in-law had heard and received Jesus because the old man had asked all the family to come into his hospital room, told them what he had done, and asked them to forgive him for the way he had lived his life. God is still opening deaf ears to hear the gospel. What an incredible God we serve!

I will share one more incident concerning an older couple in the community. Del and Roxy Williamson had been friends of Donnie's parents and had known Donnie from his birth. They had no children or family of their own. Roxy was in the hospital, and Donnie went to see her. He began sharing the gospel, but her dinner came, and it was clear this was not the time.

> God is still opening deaf ears
> to hear the gospel.
> What an incredible God we serve!

Soon she went home, and when Donnie called and asked to go see them, Roxy said yes. When he shared the gospel that day, both she and Del prayed to receive the Lord.

Donnie went to see them each week after that to have a little Bible study using the Book of John. Roxy would lovingly stroke the pages of her Bible and say, "Oh, I never knew these things." She died before long, and Del followed a few years later. Their attorney called and told us the church was in their will for $30,000. That came at a very strategic time in our church's building process, but that is another story.

# Chapter Twelve
# Church Growth and Staff Difficulties

People are hungry for biblical, expository preaching. The church began to grow as many came to a saving knowledge of the Lord Jesus Christ, were baptized, and added to the church. People were coming out from Corvallis, Albany, and areas all around. In no time, we had to go to two services.

We turned the interior of the church completely around, using the entryway for the preaching platform and thus making more room for seating. We were bursting at the seams. An addition had been built, but that was for the kitchen, the fellowship hall, and classrooms. There was no room for expansion, and since the church sat on the bank of the Willamette River, the county would not allow a permit for an additional septic system.

It was at that time that Gary Keen, one of our elders, and his wife, Pat, found an empty school building on McFarland Road near Tangent, a little community south of Albany. It was decided that we would rent the building, make a few changes to create a sanctuary, and move there. And that is what we did. Some were not happy about leaving the little country church, so a few months after moving the entire congregation to McFarland, a couple of elders returned to Peoria and formed a group there.

Since they needed to retain the name Peoria Community Church and it no longer fit us, we at Tangent decided on the name Grace

Bible Fellowship. *Grace* and *Bible* and *fellowship* were what we stood for. We found a man who would serve as pastor of the Peoria group, and we continued to grow at the McFarland location.

With growth came growing pains. We added another staff member. When he left to pursue his doctoral degree, we replaced him with another staff person (let's call him Fred). Soon, Fred became unhappy with his job responsibilities. We had taken him and his wife with us to Bend to discuss with a youth/family pastor there what we needed at Grace Bible Fellowship. He seemed to be in step with the role and assignment. But as time passed, he became more and more dissatisfied with his job description. It had not been clearly written out on paper, which was a mistake.

He even told someone in the church that he didn't have a job description and was confused about his role, his function, and what was expected of him. We did not know he said this until years later. Apparently, he had totally forgotten what we talked about in the very beginning with the man in Bend.

When Donnie and I returned from a week away, we began to hear there was growing discontent developing around Fred and a Bible study group he was leading. It had been discussed at a board meeting while we were gone. Apparently, Fred wanted to be doing the preaching and thought he should take a group of the congregation and start his own church.

A board member counseled Donnie to say nothing when the board reconvened. During that board meeting, those who had been voicing discontent began to change their tune. Yet the discontent continued. Donnie struggled. He was a very gentle, peaceful man. If the Lord wanted him to leave Grace Bible Fellowship, he would obey. Was that what God wanted him to do?

We met with a church in a community a hundred miles away who had contacted us to consider pastoring there. We even wrote a letter of resignation, but Mr. Powell, the pastoral theology teacher at Prairie Bible Institute, had told his prospective pastors that if it ever came to that, they were to put the letter in their desk and pray about it.

And that is what we did. Only our adult children knew about the letter. We took one week to do nothing but pray and read the word of God. Our goal was to read through the entire Bible—Old and New Testaments—in that week and see what God would say. We did nothing but read and pray. (I would never suggest that, however, as a good way to read the Bible, but that was our plan for then.)

At the end of that week, Donnie was told three things. First, he was not released from Grace Bible Fellowship. Second, he was to preach the word. That had been his focus since he began pastoring—expository preaching. And, finally, he was to invest in those who wanted to do the work of the ministry. His motto from the time he started preaching came from Ephesians 4:12. The Lord had given him to the church as a pastor/teacher *"for the equipping of the saints for the work of the ministry, for the edifying of the body of Christ."* This was the Scripture on the front of every church bulletin.

Although people with personal issues would come to him for counsel, that was not to distract him from his primary assignment. Good expository preaching requires hours of preparation. If individuals came with personal problems, he would meet with them and then direct them to one of two Christian counselors in the area for additional help, if needed. If Donnie were to give himself to the work of preaching and other pastoral ministries, he could not be distracted with hours of counseling. If finances were an issue for these people, the church would subsidize the cost. This approach was more efficient and cost-effective than hiring a full-time therapist or filling up his time with counseling.

So how was the discontent with the youth and family pastor resolved? It continued for a time, but it was finally decided in an elders' meeting that Fred should be released from Grace Bible

Fellowship. The decision fell to Donnie as senior pastor, and it was difficult for him. He hated any kind of dissension, and we did love Fred and his family.

We had been involved in their lives since they had come to Christ and in their subsequent training at Prairie Bible Institute. But it was agreed by everyone that this was the only reasonable solution. Donnie had tried to make Fred content by finding more work for him. Eventually, though, he became more of a distraction to the work of the ministry than an asset and took more of Donnie's thoughts and time than could be justified.

There were certain families who left the church, which was very painful for Donnie and me because they were some of the ones we had invested in the most over many years. Divisiveness in any fellowship is a grievous thing. The church gave Fred and his family a generous severance pay and continued to pay his insurance until he was able to find another source of income. Years later, he returned to Donnie to seek forgiveness for the turmoil he had caused the church. In the interim, he had become a pastor at another church and then realized what he had put Donnie through.

I did not have any animosity toward Fred's wife, but eventually she came to me to seek forgiveness and reconciliation. As a demonstration of love and respect, she asked me to be the speaker at a ladies' retreat she orchestrated for her church. What a sweet relationship we have had with that couple over the ensuing years. I am confident that God is pleased when His people resolve issues and share that kind of love.

## Chapter Thirteen
## Building Issues and Budget

Grace Bible Fellowship was still renting from the school, but eventually, the school district decided to sell the building. Did we want to buy it? We knew the problems it had and felt the price was too high. After we had been there six and a half years, someone from the school district called to say they had sold the property and that we had one month to relocate.

That was when we found a Seventh-Day Adventist church in Albany that was willing to rent their facility to us for Sunday services. Occasionally, they would have a wedding on Sunday, and we would have to beat the bushes to find a place for Sunday worship. We met in various grange halls, at the senior center, and wherever we could find a place on short notice. The board meetings, various small meetings, and a women's Bible study I taught all met at our home. We had sold our home on the farm and were living in a new home we had built on Easy Avenue in Albany, so accessibility for our people was not a problem.

About that same time, Donnie organized some planning meetings that met at the Millersburg city hall. Along with a number of leaders from the church, we worked for several days outlining who we were as a church and developing a purpose statement. Donnie felt it was in connection with this strategizing that church growth exploded. It was obvious that we needed a building of our own for the church. We had some money in the building fund, and we knew who we were as a church and how God wanted us to minister.

A piece of property just down McFarland Road from the elementary school we had rented was a perfect location, but when we inquired about it, the owner was not interested in selling. Donnie and the board looked at more than 30 properties, but nothing else seemed to fit or work out.

Marion Knox farmed that property we wanted on McFarland Road. One day, he received a call from the owner who said she woke up that morning and decided she wanted to sell that acreage to the church. Her accountant had suggested she sell something, and she was ready to move on it. She had 16 acres and wanted to sell us eight for $60,000.

When we did some research, we learned that the land was zoned rural residential five (RR5) and could be divided into three pieces of five acres each. Each piece would then be worth a minimum of $50,000. We felt we had to be honest with the owner and tell her what she had. She could realize more profit by dividing the property into fives. But, no, she wanted to sell the eight acres, the very heart of the watermelon, to the church. Who do you suppose woke her up that morning with that determination? Thank You, Jesus!

We purchased the property, but we still needed a building. We had some money in the building fund but not nearly enough to build an adequate church. With Marion Knox's help, church building plans were drawn up. The big question was whether we should borrow. Again, it was Marion who suggested that we not settle that issue at the time but simply start building with the funds we had. And that is what we did.

Many remember the day we all parked our cars at the McFarland School and marched down the road to dedicate the property and have a groundbreaking ceremony. We had a number of small spades, and everyone who wanted to dug a shovelful of dirt, signifying ownership.

We all held hands as we stood in a circle, thanking God and dedicating the property and ourselves to His service.

So the building construction began. Cement flooring and the foundation were laid. The framing was done. The beautiful laminated wood beams were donated by a Christian mill owner. Before long, the roof was up and the outside siding was completed. Doors and windows were in place. The building was enclosed and much was accomplished, but we were still renting the Seventh-Day Adventist church. We were out of money and far from having the new facility livable for a church congregation, and the county would not allow it to be used as such. Thousands of dollars were sitting there in an uninhabitable building. It was time to make a move.

## Miraculous Financial Provision

It was time for another amazing miracle in which the entire congregation would be involved. We started what was called the "Time to Move" campaign. Donnie presented the idea to the board, and all of them said, "Let's go for it."

I remember Donnie coming home from that board meeting saying, "What have I done?" He knew the burden of putting this together and pulling it off would be on his shoulders. Yet he knew God was in it and that He would be the one pulling it off.

Donnie, with the help of Marion Knox, our construction supervisor, figured we would need $120,000 just to finish the bare bones construction enough for the county to permit us to occupy the building. Someone designed a beautiful, full-color brochure celebrating all that God had already done for us in the building process and what plans He had for us going forward. It outlined how far we had come with the building, what was still needed, and how people could have an impact and leave a legacy for their children. About a fourth of the church was recruited to take the brochures to the homes of the other three-fourths to explain our proposal.

The plan was to have a special offering for the building on a designated day in May. On that day, people were asked to indicate what God was asking them to pledge to give to the building fund in the next eight months, over and above their regular giving. They were asked to pray as a family during the next six or seven weeks before that day in May when the cash offering and pledges would be received.

During those weeks, Donnie preached sermons on faith, hope, love, service, thanksgiving, and generosity. I especially remember his message on how to prepare for a miracle. He used the Scripture about Christ feeding the 5,000 with five loaves and two fish given by the small boy. Do you suppose others were there with lunches? What an incredible story that kid had to tell when he went home. He had given what he had, and Jesus had fed the multitudes. I would bet that he was profoundly impacted by that experience and his life was never the same. Do you suppose he took home one of those baskets of leftovers? Who knows? Give what you have and watch God multiply it.

As I have said, Donnie did not like to know who was giving what. Nor did he like to tell others about our giving, which had always been very generous. But because of David's example in 1 Chronicles 29, we felt we must be the example for our people. David had enumerated what he would give for building the temple, and then he asked the leaders and the people what the Lord would have them give.

Because it had been determined that $120,000 was needed to finish the building just enough to occupy it, Donnie and I agreed we would trust the Lord for 10 percent of that. That was a huge commitment and stretch of faith on our part. When Donnie shared that, it became a major incentive to the people to trust God for what He would have them give and pledge. I heard from several that they adjusted their giving decision when they realized what

## Building Issues and Budget

we were doing. If leaders expect their people to trust the Lord and sacrifice, they must do the same.

A home devotional relating to the sermons for those weeks was prepared along with a coloring book for smaller children. Everyone was to be involved. People were encouraged to share how God was providing the funds they had agreed, by faith, to give. Excitement was building.

The day of the offering arrived. A wheel barrel carrying the offering from the children was rolled down the aisle. Those funds were to be used for a playground. I remember my granddaughter Alyssa beaming from ear to ear. She was just a little girl but had somehow saved up and given $100. The offering was gathered that morning, and the plan was to meet that evening at the unfinished building to announce the total. Remember, we were praying and believing for $120,000 in cash and pledges.

Donnie had spray-painted some bricks to look like gold bricks. For drama, he planned to have the people count with him by $10,000 as he stacked each brick. We had brought in folding chairs and set them up for the gathering. When the treasurer told him the total, he realized he did not have enough bricks to count by $10,000.

Our adult children and their spouses were sitting in the front row and knew their dad's plan for drama with the gold bricks. When he began counting by $20,000 per brick instead of $10,000, their mouths dropped open, and they began to elbow each other. God had done beyond even our wildest dreams. The cash offering was $159,224, and the pledges would bring the total beyond $340,000. That would be enough to not only occupy the building but also to carpet the whole building, build a sound booth, purchase sound equipment, and do all the things needed as well as some we had not even envisioned. We finished and moved into the building in September the following year, debt-free. Isn't God exceedingly, abundantly beyond amazing?

In October, we presented the drama *Heaven's Gates & Hell's Flames*, which proved to be a very powerful evangelistic tool. Donnie had contacted Bible-teaching churches in the area and invited them to bring their people and be part of the follow-up. The first night we had to turn away crowds. The next night was packed, too, and we announced we would have an additional, unplanned performance to accommodate those who still wanted to bring unsaved friends and family.

I spoke just recently to a woman who found Christ during those meetings. She was at church watching her granddaughter get baptized. The ripple effect goes on. How awesome is our God!

## More Growing Pains

Our sanctuary was adequate, but we soon realized we were hurting for classrooms for our children and youth ministries. Someone with vision for our ministry donated $50,000 to purchase and place on the property a double-wide building with two large rooms for classrooms. But in a few years, we realized we needed to build an addition to the building to accommodate our children and Sunday school classes.

We prayed and then followed a similar giving campaign called "Time to Expand." We believed we needed about $350,000 to build what was needed. I remember people being excited about this new project. The earlier campaign had been such a faith builder. Again, Donnie and I prayed and believed God was prompting us to trust Him for 10 percent. We had no idea where that amount would come from, but God was leading us to step out in faith.

And again, God did more than we had envisioned. The offering on May 22, 2005, in cash and in pledges over the following seven months totaled $500,624.76. Amazing! Cash from adults was $272,872.89; from the youth came $1,912.26; and the children contributed $1,475.41. Adults pledged $224,277 and the children another $88.00.

## Building Issues and Budget

Since we went over the $350,000, we were able to not only finish the ministry center but also make sure it was set up to be efficient and effective. We were also able to remodel part of the west wing for some much-needed office space and a library. What a praise service we had Sunday evening when the results were announced! We were created to give God glory and praise. People were encouraged to watch to see how God would bless them.

I might add here that the financial statement always looked healthy. We never had what is called a budget. When there was a need and the funds were available, it was up to either the elders or the entire board to decide what to do. We had always subsidized family camp, the women's retreat, and other events to enable everyone to attend.

A financial statement was included in the bulletin each month. At the annual meeting, a comprehensive yearly financial statement was printed and explained by the financial secretary, but the church never made a budget for the coming year. Who knew what was coming? Besides, each year was different from the previous year. God generally leads by putting a light on our path and directing our steps instead of giving us a road map. That doesn't mean a church shouldn't make plans. When God was leading in the plans, the finances were generally available.

Because of the national economic crisis in 2008, Donnie's plan was to be very careful about unessential church spending. Because our kids were grown and our expenses were down, he and I had privately decided we would take a pay cut if the need arose because he always wanted to be sure that members of the staff were covered financially. That need never arose. When Donnie died in 2009, the balance in the general fund was more than $100,000.

In the early years of our ministry, our salary had been quite meager. As time passed, however, the church paid us more generously. When we sold the farm and moved to Albany, we determined to spend every dime of the proceeds for reinvestment. That was when we began to purchase rental properties. When I lost Donnie in 2009, I was able to retire the mortgage on our home with the life insurance money and continue my life, debt-free. Surely God's blessing has always been upon us financially.

Here is the principle: If one gives to God by the shovelful, He gives back by the shovelful. The difference is that He has a bigger shovel. You can never outgive God. He blesses in one way or another.

> *"Bring all the tithes into the storehouse,*
> *That there may be food in My house,*
> *And try Me now in this,"*
> Says the LORD of hosts.
> *"If I will not open for you the windows of heaven*
> *And pour out for you such blessing*
> *That there will not be room enough to receive it"* (emphasis added).
>
> —Malachi 3:10

Rarely are we to *try the Lord*, but this is one time we are counseled to do so. God has shown Himself to be abundantly faithful to His word in this area in our lives.

Here is another Scripture along this line:

> *This Book of the Law shall not depart from your mouth, but you shall meditate in it day and night, that you may observe to do according to all that is written in it. For then you will make your way prosperous, and then you will have* good success (emphasis added).
>
> —Joshua 1:8

Many may achieve success, but not *good success*. What is the difference? Men often sacrifice their wives, their families, or their walks with God to have success in their business and financial pursuits. They may achieve success and become wealthy, but it is not good success if it costs them their families or their salvation. Be very wise, my children. God cannot be mocked. We reap what we sow (Gal. 6:7).

Over the years, God truly blessed our ministry in remarkable ways. Gratefulness and praise were constantly on our lips. Scripture says that God inhabits the praises of His people (Ps. 22:3 KJV).

That is another principle. If you want to experience His presence, learn to praise Him. Avoid murmuring and complaining like the plague. By praising, you fulfill the purpose for which you were created. Many say they want to know God's will, God's plan for their lives. That is a good goal; however, much of His purpose is revealed clearly in the Scriptures. First Thessalonians 5:18 says, *"In everything give thanks; for this is the will of God in Christ Jesus for you."* It does not say we are to give thanks *for* all things but *in* all things. That is an acknowledgment that we know God is ultimately *in* all things; He is sovereign.

> Gratefulness is a choice.

Somehow, when we trust Him, knowing He is bigger than any circumstance, we can know He will bring everything together for our good and growth and also for His glory. God loves it when we are grateful and thankful, and so do other people. It is much easier and more pleasant to live with a grateful person than with one who always sees and dwells on the negative. Gratefulness is a choice.

## Chapter Fourteen
## Equipping the Saints

Donnie lived by the assignment God had given him from Ephesians 4:11–12: *"And He Himself gave some to be . . . pastors and teachers, for the equipping of the saints for the work of the ministry, for the edifying of the body of Christ."* His job was not to do all of the ministering. He was to equip the saints to do the work of the ministry. Occasionally, he would say from the pulpit, "Now, who are the ministers?" The answer, of course, was "We are."

Sometimes, individuals suggested we should have a certain ministry in the church. Donnie would ask if they were proposing to take on, organize, and lead such a ministry. The suggested plan sometimes appropriately fit our program, but without leadership, a ministry was never started.

Harry Hanson with his wife, Marge, both now with the Lord, initiated a program for senior adults dubbed "Saints Alive," which is continuing to bless our seniors to this day. The older members of our body are encouraged to meet in a back room of a Sizzler restaurant that is reserved one Wednesday per month. Concerns and prayer requests are explained, and a speaker provides a message.

It was also Harry who proposed a program where every person in the church would be lifted up in prayer every week. It was a simple list with no person having more than five people or families to cover, and yet each person in the church would be wrapped in prayer every week.

Because we had the equipment to do so, Donnie's sermons were audiotaped and videotaped. Harry made it his ministry to take copies of the audiotapes to a nearby truck stop and restaurant to make them available for free to truckers or anyone else who might want to listen to them.

Ed Knox, hired as our music minister, counselor, and pastoral assistant, had spent 18 years working at KWIL, the local Christian radio station, before coming on staff at Grace Bible Fellowship. When it was decided to put Donnie's messages on the radio, Ed had the skills to edit and prepare them to each fill the time of two radio broadcasts. That required two and a half sermons to fill the five days of each week. Since we had a backlog of years of sermons on audiotape, there were enough to last until after Donnie went to be with the Lord. Donnie called his radio broadcasts *Journeys in the Word*. Many were challenged, edified, and blessed through this ministry.

### Dying with Grace

For 31 years, Donnie had taught his people how to live. The fall of 2007 brought a new challenge. He was given the task of teaching them how to die. He turned out to be an incredible example of endurance, courage, faith, and trust during the uncertain days of fighting a rare form of cancer.

We first thought the problem was a toothache. After the suspect tooth was pulled, the pain continued and worsened with no relief. A return to the dental surgeon assured us that no bone or tooth residue remained to cause the pain.

Eventually, the diagnosis was trigeminal neuralgia. It is defined as a stripping of the protective covering of the trigeminal (three-pronged) nerves that come down through the cheek from the area around the ear. When stripped of their protective covering, these nerves are super sensitive, and the result is incredible pain similar to an ongoing toothache. Donnie said he understood why it was called the suicide condition—death is preferable to hour after hour of pain.

When our dear Dr. Petersen visited with Donnie in the church parking lot, he immediately secured an emergency appointment with a neurologist. That doctor sent Donnie immediately for an MRI, and by the afternoon, we were at an appointment with an ear, nose, and throat specialist who took a biopsy accessed through his nose.

Just that quickly we learned he had a malignant, inoperable skull tumor. It was not in the brain, but it encased the carotid artery and the optic nerve, and surgery would result in blindness or death.

Frantically, we researched the best approach to treatment, and with the help of the oral surgeon who had removed the tooth, we opted to go to a doctor in Portland who was touted as having a unique approach to treating this type of tumor. I am reluctant to name him because he persuaded us to approach it with conventional treatment, and his carelessness with Donnie's case eventually convinced us of the necessity to change doctors.

Unbelievably, heavy-duty chemotherapy did shrink the tumor and relieve the pain, thank the Lord. Eventually, tests indicated that the skull tumor was gone. No cancer was detected in the lymph nodes, but to make sure, the doctors insisted on radiation treatment for the lymph nodes in his neck nearest to where the cancer had been.

Thus began the horrible process of receiving tomotherapy treatments, a very precise but strong radiation, on the dear man's neck. The result was a horrendous burn that required daily dressing, the most difficult exercise for me. But that amazing man never complained.

Because swallowing became so difficult and painful, a shunt was surgically installed into his stomach so he could be fed through a tube. He was weak and shaky and could not hold the liquid food, so that was also my assignment, which I more than gladly did.

Sadly, the cancer spread to his bones, one of the most painful forms of cancer. We learned it had spread through the blood, not the lymph nodes. All that burning of his neck was for nothing.

Many times as a pastor's wife I would struggle to discern what specifically my assignment was. During the two years of Donnie's cancer, I had no question concerning my mission. I knew my calling was to care for this amazing man and leave no stone unturned in my search to find an answer for this rare form of cancer.

Eventually, we knew hospice would be needed to manage the pain. Donnie knew what that meant from his experience with dying parishioners. Hospice does not step in until a person no longer has doctor appointments or any available treatment options.

He had the last radiation treatment on his hip and back on a Tuesday, a last-ditch effort to keep the pain at bay as long as possible. Our friends John and Sue Powell showed up in the hospital parking lot that day to help me ease him into the wheelchair for his move into the radiation facility. I had no idea they would be there, and they insisted on waiting through the treatment to help me with the painful return into the car. Money cannot buy friendships like that.

Hospice came on Wednesday with their supply of pain pills. The hospital bed was to arrive that evening.

As we waited that afternoon, his three adult daughters were curled up near him on our big king-sized bed. With his precious, weakened arms held up, together they sang the chorus "I Love You, Lord." That picture will forever be a precious memory for them and for me.

I was dreading weeks of horrendous bone pain to come. I remembered stories of some adult sons in our community being angry with God over watching their father groan and scream with the pain of bone cancer before he was relieved in death.

The bed was set up in the family room, and as we were helping Donnie into the wheelchair to move him to the hospital bed, something happened. We do not know if it was a stroke or a heart attack, but we panicked and called Ed Knox from the church to come and help us get him into the bed.

It was clear that this was a new turn in his condition. By early the next morning, Thanksgiving morning, November 26, 2009, just before a glorious sunrise, God called His remarkable servant home. God is so gracious. His precious child was spared more pain. *"Precious in the sight of the LORD is the death of His saints"* (Ps. 116:15).

Here is a portion of the letter he wrote to his church family when he knew he was going home soon. It was included in his beautiful memorial folder put together by our dear friend John Waleusiac.

My Dear Church Family,

I want to thank you for allowing me to be your pastor these many years. What a privilege and blessing God has given me, a simple farm boy. My dependency has been always upon Him, and He has never failed me. Everywhere I have gone I have been able to brag about you, my people. Together we have been a beacon to our community, not perfect but always shining out the good news of the gospel of our precious Jesus.

You know I love you all and have always known you love me. One day you will have a new pastor. Love and support him as you have loved and supported me.

Please take care of my family and precious wife. Without her support and sacrificial love, I would not have made it through these many years.

With all my love,<br>Pastor Don

PS: Thank you for all your prayers. Please don't stop now.

Married almost 50 years, my great blessing was to pastor alongside such an extraordinary servant of the Lord Jesus Christ. We had tried everything, but ultimately, the cancer took him. But the cancer did not win. Because of his faith in Jesus, he was victorious; he was an overcomer. It was our loss, but he won!

## Chapter Fifteen
## My Brokenness, My Story

After my husband's death, I wrote almost 25,000 words of this manuscript outlining incredible miracles and leadings in my husband's life and in my own, and then I stopped. I knew that was not the whole story. Thirty years earlier, a shattering discovery had hit me. I did not like that part of the story and did not want to or know how to write about it even 30 years later. That part of my story was painful and difficult.

At a women's conference at Champion Church in March 2017, Terri Savelle Foy, that year's guest speaker, challenged me to renew my dream of writing my story. I knew I was commissioned by God to pick it up and finish. I knew I had to write of my brokenness, pain, failure, and devastation for two reasons.

First, how could I write about all the incredibly positive workings of God in my life and imply that I had experienced no pain or heartbreak? To lead my readers to believe that Christians do not experience incredibly painful events and issues would be totally misleading. Was I some little cosmic pet who never experienced anguish or grief? At that point, I realized that I had to tell all of my story.

Second, my heart was to share that God is a God of restoration, healing, and redemption. I stand amazed at our bodies. We get sick, and little white blood cells are sent out to make us well. Incredible wounds are sewn up and healed. Even completely broken bones can be placed back together, encased in a cast, and often end up stronger than ever.

My goal is to convince you that broken hearts can also be healed. We have a champion, a hero, who wants to come to our rescue in these parts of our lives. No healing is greater than the healing God works in our hearts. God has given people a free will, a sacred gift He will not violate, and much of the pain and suffering comes from the choices of fallen human beings. God is sovereign and can give beauty for ashes, but ashes there will be.

At the time of my discovery, I felt like a time bomb had been dropped into my gut, waiting to explode. My world had stopped, but everything else kept going on around me. People were going to see the July 4 fireworks. Did no one realize the world had shifted on its axis? It was July, and the sun was brightly shining almost in mockery of what was happening in my heart. Could this be true, or was it a bad nightmare from which I could awaken?

Immediately after my painful discovery, I had to go with my husband to dinner at the home of a couple in our church. Donnie was the pastor, and it was too late to beg off. My mind was raging, and I remember the struggle to keep the bottled-up explosion in check throughout the evening. This was not a safe place to vent. Was there any safe place to vent, to erupt?

Have you ever felt like you were holding in a primordial scream? I remember fighting to keep a lid on that sensation throughout the evening. The anguish was bottled up. Within one minute after we left, I was exploding in rage and then dissolving into sobs.

I am sure I should have been asking God what He wanted me to do with this mess. We had had so many miracles in our lives. He is the God who is renowned for turning tragedy into triumph and messes into miracles. But I was not asking God what He wanted me to learn at this point. I was just trying to survive, to make some sense of what had happened.

Isn't that our desperate plea, to make sense of what is happening? *"Blessed are those who mourn"* (Matt. 5:4). That sounds good in theory but not so much when you are in the midst of a painful reality. When you smash your finger, you rarely say, "Thank you, Lord!" In fact, some other choice words usually spring to mind involuntarily. I was drowning in confusion and pain wondering what was next and where God was in all of this.

Of course, I was asking, *Why?* That is always the big question. Everyone wants to know why, and that starts when we are children. Children want to know why we do something. When we explain, they ask again, "Why?" Why this and why that. We get weary and finally end up saying, "Because I say so, that's why."

Can we conclude that it is natural to ask *Why?* There are some truly big questions. Why do good children die and some old cranky people live on and on? Why is there child abuse? Why do children get cancer? Why is there molestation of children, rape, murder? If God is good, and He is, why is there so much suffering?

All the things I thought were true were now in question. If I had had any smug, easy answers to life's pain and confusion, those answers were now suspect or gone. All I knew for sure was that God was my creator, Jesus was my Savior, and He would have to bring me—us—through this tragedy. I kept searching for just the right verse, the right decision, the right answer, and the right thought that would fix this, that would fix me and make the pain go away. Was this disaster my fault? What did we do wrong? What had I done wrong?

## Slow Learner

I am ashamed to confess that my recovery from this brokenness took more time than it should have, but God has been gracious, and healing and restoration have come. And, yes, I have learned and benefited from the experience in many ways. The needed refining process in my life felt like a rasping with rough sandpaper at times, or like being put into a tumbler with blocks to remove my splintery sharp edges. He was the potter, and I was the clay going round and round on the wheel. I guess I have used some mixed metaphors—a tumbler, a wheel—but appropriately so. I was a confused heap at the time.

So to say that I know what it means to have a broken heart is an understatement. This was not pain that dissolved in weeks or even months. As devastating as my discovery of breast cancer and my husband's cancer and death some years later have been, the pain was not even comparable to this heartbreak. His death meant widowhood for me, but ultimate glory for him. It was normal, understandable suffering. I will soon follow. This heartbreak was none of those things.

## Unspeakable Pain: To Tell or Not to Tell?

I have struggled with the decision to share the details of my anguish. How could I be honest and transparent and yet keep the details of such a major event covered up? Those outside the church love to reproach church people as being nothing but a bunch of hypocrites. I had never been a person who pretended to be something I wasn't. I know that honesty and openness about my flaws as well as my strengths are required in order to be approachable.

But here I was, a fraud, a phony, trying to hide, to conceal, the unspeakable pain I was going through. Is that even Christian? Does that make me a hypocrite, a Pharisee?

Unspeakable pain! *Unspeakable*! Ahh, that was the rub. I was caught between the need to scream about my pain, and knowing that to do so would betray others. How could I throw others under the bus to satisfy my need for understanding, validation, healing, and support?

That was 30 years ago, but what about today as I write? I have been given reluctant permission to reveal the details by some of those most deeply involved, but is it wise to strip others to nakedness and bare their issues before the world? That is their decision, not mine. The world is not a safe or kind or benign place.

I had written a whole chapter for this book revealing the details of what had occurred and how that discovery had devastated me, but those involved did not feel good about that chapter. So I could not find peace about such a public revelation.

A verse in Colossians has often been a key to difficult questions in my decision making. *"And let the peace of God* rule *in your hearts . . . and be thankful"* (Col. 3:15, emphasis added). In sports, the referee rules. When he blows the whistle, everything stops. He rules; he is in charge. Until the referee is satisfied, the game does not proceed. He makes his ruling, and then the game can continue.

When a person does not have peace about a decision or action, everything should stop. Lack of peace has blown the whistle, and we must let God's peace rule. Until the needed peace is restored, one should not move forward. Let the peace of God rule; be the referee.

I had written many pages about the details of my overwhelming discovery. But since I did not have peace about it, I knew God was speaking. I had no peace until those pages were erased. Then I found the peace I needed to proceed.

You are no doubt thinking, *If you are not going to share the details of your anguish, why on earth are you talking about it at all?* Good question. But the answer is easy. I want to scream to the world that God can bring healing, restoration, and victory to the hearts and minds and lives that have been shattered. I take comfort in the fact that the apostle Paul did not give the details of his thorn in the flesh but simply said, *"My grace is sufficient for you"* (2 Cor. 12:9). I had thought I needed to write the sensational details so people would want to read my story. But God said no, you need to write truth so people will find healing from your story.

## The Heart of My Story

This is the heart of my story. I am convinced God has put Isaiah 61 on my heart. I believe He has commissioned me *"to preach good tidings to the poor; He has sent me to heal the brokenhearted, to proclaim liberty to the captives, and the opening of the prison to those who are bound"* (Isa. 61:1).

I am totally aware that this passage is a prophecy about Jesus. He stood up in the synagogue in Nazareth, read this passage and then announced, *"Today this Scripture is fulfilled in your hearing"* (Luke 4:21). I believe that as His body, His church, and His bride, however, we are commissioned to continue the work He did while we are here on Earth.

As I revisit those days, I recognize that at that time, I could see no redemptive value in what happened. How could my children's faith and walk with the Lord have benefited? How was my life's influence enhanced? But especially how could God's glory be magnified?

As a believer in the amazing redemptive power of Christ, I hang on to the firm conviction that He can use even the worst Satan dishes out for our refining and growth and for His glory and honor. God uses damaged, broken, sinful people for His work because that is all He has. He is the God who specializes in giving *"beauty for ashes, the oil of joy for mourning, the garment of praise for the spirit of heaviness"* (Isa. 61:3).

Why does He do this? Why does He want to restore us to joy and victory? *"That they may be called trees of righteousness, the planting of the LORD, that He may be glorified"* (Isa. 61:3, emphasis added).

I have learned that our greatest anguish comes not from what happens to us but from what happens to those we love, those closest to us. I had always told myself not to get too caught up in ministry. My family—my children—was my first priority. My ministry and my message would grow out of my ministry to them, but here was a situation that involved them about which I was not free to speak.

> God uses damaged, broken, sinful people for His work because that is all He has.

I would like to say I handled my grief in a very mature, godly way, but I did not. That was not my concern. My concern was for my children. For me, it was to simply survive. My husband kept insisting I was not a failure. The fact that each one has been able to transcend their experience and to maintain their love of the Lord is a testament that something was being done right and that God was more than faithful. But I was not feeling that then. They are beautiful, accomplished, and amazing people. I am so proud of them. Yes, all have had their own struggles, but life is difficult for everyone, isn't it?

The few very close friends I confided in were not helpful. They couldn't be. There was no fixing the situation or my broken heart. I am sure they wanted to help, but words were often more painful than silence. If the wrong word was said, a sense of failure, hopelessness, and self-condemnation would flood over me. I would want to be alone, but then the aloneness would become so lonely. The most helpful support came from one cousin who simply cried. My rage was like a bottled-up volcano ready to explode. I went from grief, to uncontrollable sobbing, to screaming into a pillow.

The Bible story about Mary and her alabaster box fascinated me, and I had taught it to others several times. She poured out her overflowing love to Jesus as she sat at His feet. In order to anoint

His feet with the very costly ointment, she had to break the box, a valuable item in itself. Of course, Judas, who kept the money bag, was indignant about such a waste. *"For it might have been sold . . . and given to the poor"* (Mark 14:5). The Gospel of Mark says that even some of the other disciples were indignant.

A beautiful aspect of the story is that when the bottle was broken, the fragrance of the poured-out ointment filled the room. Without the broken flask, there would have been no anointing, no fragrance.

Jesus said the poor would always be with them, so leave her alone. She had anointed Him for His burial, and wherever the gospel went, this story of Mary would go, too. Incidentally, Mary was the only one who anointed Jesus before His burial. What a beautiful story! I believed I was willing to be broken and poured out because of my love for Jesus. I thought so. That had been my claim.

But my source of brokenness was beyond anything I could imagine. I never visualized that my brokenness would include my whole family. And where was the fragrance? This situation had no sweet aroma. Little did I know what brokenness would cost me and those whom I loved. But I was broken, devastated, shattered. *Where are you, Jesus? I am drowning here.* That pretty much described my questions and feelings at the time. Little did I comprehend the depth and richness of my relationship with Jesus that would grow from this time of brokenness.

# Chapter Sixteen
# Help for Healing

My poor husband did not totally understand the depth of my pain. So he finally took me to see our dear Dr. Glenn Petersen. Dr. Glenn was very understanding and appreciative of my pain, and he put me on an antidepressant. Now, dear readers, if you think that good, spirit-filled Christians should never need to take such medication, blessings on you. But do any of you take blood pressure meds, cholesterol meds, or thyroid meds? Why is it appropriate to take medicines for other conditions but unspiritual to take medicine for a broken heart?

Brokenness! The source of my brokenness had no fragrance. Perhaps a soothing aroma can come from the broken places in our hearts. Could love, compassion, gentleness, and understanding flow more abundantly from a heart that has been broken open? I do believe I have become more gentle. Jesus said, *"The thief does not come except to steal, and to kill, and to destroy. I have come that they may have life, and that they may have it more abundantly"* (John 10:10). The thief stole, but because of Jesus's mercy, life has come, and it has come *more abundantly*.

## Helpful Medication

I so thank the Lord for the six months on antidepressants and how I was able to survive. I still thought every day—it seemed like all the time—about what had happened, but I didn't have to talk about it. I could keep it inside. I could sleep, although fitfully. Dr. Petersen said he would prescribe medication, but we needed to find some Christian counseling, too.

We did find a counselor. We went one time, and then she moved away. She told Donnie she thought he was in denial, that he was out of touch with his feelings. For weeks, he kept denying that he was in denial, claiming he was simply not a very emotive person. Since we never went for any other therapy, I finally said, "Okay, okay. You are not stuffing your feelings. You are not in denial."

That worked until he started having panic attacks. Oh, maybe she was right. The answer for him was to cut back on caffeine and so many early mornings and late nights working. Donnie did not particularly enjoy counseling, so we never found another counselor.

The antidepressants worked. I survived. I was calm. Life went on for six months until we went back to Dr. Petersen. He suggested that it was probably time for me to wean off the medication. I agreed. He said to go off the 150 cc dose slowly, to drop 25 cc every few days. That sounded good. I did not like the medication anyway. It gave me a dry mouth, and Donnie said I snored. Ha!

In a few weeks, I was off the medication, and I became totally obsessive-compulsive, totally nuts. I could not sleep. I could not sit still. I was constantly busy doing something I thought needed to be done. My windows and house had never been so clean. Since I couldn't sleep, I would go grocery shopping in the middle of the night. I was helping plan a 50th wedding anniversary party for a sister-in-law's folks. I was a superwoman. The sobbing would come and go. I was beside myself, of course—whatever that means. When I called the doctor to tell him what I was doing and to ask how long this would go on, he told me to have Donnie bring me in to see him.

When we entered the office, the nurse said the doctor wanted to see Donnie, and I was to sit in the waiting room. As exhausted,

## Help for Healing

paranoid, and drained as I was at this point, I panicked. They were plotting behind my back. They had secrets.

I had an extra set of car keys in my purse. I had to get out of there. Very quietly and calmly, I got up, walked as normally as I could, went to the car, and left. The doctor's private office where they were talking had a window that looked out on the street in front of the office. They looked out, saw me, and said, "Oh, my gosh! There she goes." Without a car, Donnie was stuck, and he had no idea where I was going or what to do.

As I left, I realized I had no idea where I was going, either. *Okay, I will go to my oldest daughter Sherry's office*, I thought. She worked for Randy, a personal friend from our church. I got there, hid behind Randy's inner office door sobbing, and said, "They are keeping secrets, and I am panicked." About that time Donnie was on the phone to Sherry, and I was found.

Dr. Petersen had found a Christian therapy program in a hospital in Portland. My insurance would cover therapy for four weeks if I were in a hospital. He wanted to give Donnie a check for $500 because that was required up front to enter the program.

I was so embarrassed! We went back to Dr. Glenn's office. We had not found an outpatient counselor, but this was a very professional Christian program where I could go and work through my pain.

He said it would be best if I chose to commit myself voluntarily, but he had the power to commit me if I wouldn't. *Commit*—what a terrifying word! *Committed* to a psych ward. I asked him if the doors would be locked. He said probably. Oh, no! Now I really was scared.

But I was in such pain that I was ready to trust Dr. Glenn, the Lord, and my husband. So I packed my little ditty bag with a few essentials and off I went to the fifth floor of Woodland Park Hospital somewhere in Portland, Oregon. A psychiatrist visited every day to prescribe meds and monitor the physical issues. Several psychologists did group and individual counseling and therapy every day. And yes, the doors were locked. But it was a safe place, and after the four weeks, I didn't want to leave.

## How Do We Deal with Anger?

I was so angry with my husband. I had gone on the antidepressants for six months, and he had not taken me to any therapy. Six months—wasted. Why didn't he take the stupid pills? Why didn't he commit himself to a psych ward? Ha! I don't know why I thought he should have found a counselor for me. Somehow, I felt he should have found someone he would approve and trust. That was his job, wasn't it?

Now that I had come off the antidepressant, I was exploding with anger, and he was the only safe place to direct it. I knew he would love me through this. Poor dear! When he had gotten counseling for another woman in the church, I had been furious. He would take care of her needs. What was I? Just a gnat under his saddle blanket?

I knew people had survived greater tragedy than I was experiencing. Children lost in death, children with terminal illnesses, deformed and maimed children. I was ashamed, embarrassed that I was not handling this better. What do you do with such anger? What do you do with such disappointment and pain? I did come to realize, however, that these 28 days in the hospital added up to the best-spent month of my life. I confess I handled this situation like a spiritual lightweight rather than a godly Christian woman walking in the grace God gives.

It has been difficult to share this portion of my story. We want to hide the days of our failure, our shame, and our emotional bankruptcy. We want to appear perfect, mature, and spiritual so we will be admired. But to be useful and to be loved, we must be real, genuine, and honest. My failure resulted in my spending a month in a hospital psych ward. Not pretty but true.

## Help for Healing

When we are real, we may be hurt, but the hurt and isolation of hiding and not touching anyone else's heart is a worse hurt; it is a lonely hurt. Being honest, open, and real brings healing, hope, and encouragement to ourselves and to others. And in the process, we find that we are tougher, more resilient, and more courageous than we thought. For me, personally divulging all the details of this situation would be easier. But easier is not necessarily wiser.

> Being honest, open, and real brings healing, hope, and encouragement to ourselves and to others.

## Chapter Seventeen
## What I Have Learned

We don't live in a perfect world. What might a perfect world look like? In a perfect world, chocolate would have no calories and procrastination would be honored as a virtue. Teenagers would rather clean their rooms than talk on their phones, text, or play video games. Children on a trip would say, "Isn't riding in a car fun?" And then they would go to sleep. One woman said that in a perfect world, men would go through labor with the second and fourth child, which means families would have no more than three kids. I saw a cartoon in my doctor's office that said, "Put a crouton on top of your hot fudge Sunday, and you can call it a salad."

But we don't live in a perfect world, do we? No! Stuff happens—sometimes awful, ugly, heartbreaking stuff, as I have shared. Our lives are a story, a drama with many episodes. Many, maybe most, of these chapters come with things that are out of our control.

I partly agree with melancholy Jaques in Shakespeare's play *As You Like It*. "All the world's a stage, / And all the men and women merely players: / They have their exits and their entrances; / And one man in his time plays many parts."[1] That's true. Our lives are a story, a drama. This is no dress rehearsal, and we have no stunt doubles to play the tough parts.

I was not happy with this chapter in my story. But there it was. It was not the story I wanted to experience or tell, and yet it was a major, significant, life-changing episode in my life. What was I going to do with it?

I agree with Macbeth when he says, "Life's but a walking shadow."[2] Scripture tells us our lives are but a breath, a vapor. The Psalmist prays, *"So teach us to number our days, that we may gain a heart of wisdom"* (Ps. 90:12).

But I do not agree with Macbeth's profoundly pessimistic statement that we are all but "a poor player / That struts and frets his hour upon the stage / And then is heard no more: it is a tale / Told by an idiot, full of sound and fury / Signifying nothing."[3] I do not believe God purposes our lives to be meaningless, signifying nothing. I maintain there is a bigger drama going on. God has given us a part to play, albeit a very small part. Yet it is our part, so it has great significance. We were created to "glorify God, and to enjoy him forever,"[4] according to the old Westminster catechism.

> I do not believe God purposes our lives to be meaningless, signifying nothing. I maintain there is a bigger drama going on.

It is the difficult chapters in our lives that give us the greatest opportunity to grow, be refined, and, by faith, allow God to make us trophies of His grace. *"That they may be called trees of righteousness, the planting of the LORD, that He may be glorified"* (Isa. 61:3). During those times survival depends on His amazing grace.

What did I learn? First, I learned that I had gone off the antidepressants way too quickly. The psychiatrist at the hospital said that although it was not clear in the literature, a slow withdrawal would be more like dropping 25 cc every six months, not every few days. That would give me three months to adjust and three months to coast and enjoy the equilibrium. No wonder I went bonkers. The doctor put me back on the same medication and wanted to double it. I made my case for 200 cc instead of 300 knowing how hard withdrawal would be. I did more than fine with that much and was able to do the work of therapy and find ways to cope effectively.

I will be eternally grateful to Dr. Petersen and that program. It was new and did not last very long after my stay. Knowing how healing it was for me, I was able to direct several struggling friends to the same program, but eventually the whole program was dissolved. I am convinced God had opened that program just for me at just that time. Thank You, Jesus.

Another thing I learned was the great wisdom of knowing there are no easy answers. At least I know I didn't have all the answers to life's pain, grief, hurt, and sorrow. Nor did anyone else, it seems. *Oh God, how many times have I tried to portray that I was some depository of great biblical wisdom and answers? Please forgive me!*

The answer is Jesus, *"in whom are hidden all the treasures of wisdom and knowledge"* and power and grace and healing (Col. 2:3). Notice that it is *in Him*. Simplistic platitudes and pat answers from us are often more hurtful than helpful. When someone is hurting, it is no time to beat them up with Scriptural answers and correction or rebuke. The best we can do during these deeply painful times is to be totally present, show compassion to them, listen, and usually say nothing.

I love the passage in 1 Kings 19 where Elijah is exhausted after facing down the false prophets of Baal and running from Jezebel. He is so depressed that he feels suicidal; he wants God to kill him. After declaring his depression to the Lord, he sleeps. Then the Lord has an angel wake him up and feed him. He then goes back to sleep before being awakened and fed by the angel again. Sometimes, when we are discouraged, depressed, and exhausted from the challenges and trials of life and ministry, what we need is simply to have our physical needs met; we need to sleep and eat.

## Broken and Living in the Fishbowl

Of course, everyone in the whole Willamette Valley area knew that Carol had spent time in the psych ward. I couldn't do this in my own little corner, could I? Got to love that fishbowl experience! When I ended up in the hospital, Donnie fell apart. Now he felt like a failure. He withdrew from preaching so he could pray for and minister to his wife. Everyone began asking what was wrong with me. I pled with him to get back in the pulpit as soon as he was up to it. I figured that the sooner he did, the quicker people would stop asking about me. I was squirming under the glass. Whoever "they" were, it was bothering me. Wouldn't you love to give "they" a talking to sometime?

When I was released from the hospital, older people in the community would smile, pat my back, and tell me they were sorry about my nervous breakdown. Or they would tell me about other people who had had a nervous breakdown. Oh great! How do you explain that you had simply come off your meds too fast and that you were totally thankful for this program you would not have otherwise experienced? Oh, the delights of fishbowl living as a pastor's wife in a small community!

I kept asking the counselors, "What do you do with anger?" I wanted some answers, steps I could learn and take. I had never been so angry. They were the counselors, the professionals, weren't they? No step-by-step, easy answers were given. But as I worked on my issues, the anger began to dissipate.

I learned that I had used anger to cover most of my emotions. My family of origin disapproved of anger, but it was still expressed on a regular basis. It was a useful, strong emotion. I rarely felt rejection, fear, or insecurity. I could simply get angry, and those other emotions could be repressed and not felt or realized. And as my anger began to leave, all these other emotions began to surface.

I did not particularly like this, especially feelings of rejection, insecurity, fear, and "less-than" inferiority. But I was told and began to see that to be a fully developed human, experiencing all these emotions should be part of my makeup. Anger no longer controlled or dominated all these other feelings.

My confidence did begin to return, but the process was not quick and easy. I experienced more feelings of fear, insecurity, rejection and self-doubt than I ever had. Previously, no one ever rejected me or made me feel inferior. If someone disparaged me, I would just get angry. I didn't usually display the anger, but it was a useful protective emotion to have.

I remember the self-doubt I experienced shortly after leaving the hospital when I was with a group of women from our church. I had the irrational feeling that I did not belong, that I was not included, that I was invisible, and that they did not want me there. Where did all those thoughts come from? For a period of time, I was very fragile. This was weak, puny, self-centered thinking. Eventually I grew past such debilitating thoughts.

In the months since, however, I have found myself more capable of genuine empathy and understanding. I understand how the kid who is selected last for the softball team at recess feels. Being chosen last for anything is painful. I had a better understanding of how the woman whose husband has left her feels, and how the kid whose parents are going through a divorce feels. Basically, I am more capable of recognizing the hurt in people's faces when mounting disappointments are beginning to cause them to lose hope. A person can live with almost anything except loss of hope. When one loses hope, suicide becomes a risk. The Bible speaks of faith, hope, and love, and the greatest of these is love, but hope seems to sustain the other two. Without hope, where is faith or love? Without hope, life is dead. Life is over when we lose hope.

> A person can live with almost anything except loss of hope.

## Group Therapy

I loved the hospital group therapy. I began to realize I could see and understand other people's issues better than my own. I was quite adept at discerning where others in the group had irrational thinking. Hello! I had plenty of practice since I had been processing my own issues with the same illogical reasoning. When I asked the counselor about this, she said that of course we see others' blind spots better than our own. So do therapists. That's why therapists need therapy.

Incidentally, we often gain great insight and healing from deep genuine friendships. Safe relationships or peer groups can often be as productive as professional therapy. Close, safe friendships in which we are not afraid to dig deeply into our innermost fears and anxieties can be powerfully therapeutic and healing. We need each other. But deep trust is required before we can strip and expose those deepest places and fears in our hearts.

One frightening aspect about my time in the hospital was that I was terrified of really seeing myself. I think most of us don't really know or understand ourselves, our blind spots, and our annoying personality quirks and habits. I was working very hard on me and my issues, honestly peeling off the layers of the onion one by one, so to speak. No excusing, no blaming, no rationalizing. What did I need to learn to be able to handle my grief with more maturity, insight, godliness, and a lot less hurt and pain?

The counselors even suggested I let up on myself. I didn't have to work so hard. But this was my time to learn about me. Once when Donnie visited, I was in tears as I expressed my terror at revealing myself to myself. What if I didn't like what I saw?

The biggest fear was finding that maybe what had happened in my family was really all my fault. What if I was a terrible person and didn't even know it? What if they were reaping the consequences of my sins for when I walked away from the Lord for those five years? Of course, precious man that he was, Donnie simply held me and assured me I was a good person, that I wasn't to blame, and that it was going to be okay.

David prayed in Psalm 139:23–24, "Search me, O God, and know my heart; try me, and know my anxieties; and see if there is any wicked way in me, and lead me in the way everlasting." If David needed to pray that prayer, certainly I needed to also. It was a scary prayer for me. But only with insight can we grow and change. I was desperate for that.

## No Power, No Responsibility

Another insight I gained is that I am not responsible for the things over which I have no control. People would come for counseling or advice, and if I could not "fix" them, I thought I must be a failure. Isn't that the job of a pastor's wife? If my kids experienced pain, frustration, or failure, it meant I was a failure as a parent, right? Isn't that a mom's job? If people didn't like me, there must be something wrong with me. To be a success, everyone must approve of me, right? Wrong!

I learned that these were just some of the lies we tell ourselves. I learned that if I have no power over a situation, I am not responsible for it. What a relief! Did you hear that? We are not responsible for all those things over which we have no control. I am responsible for my sin, my behavior, and my choices. That is a lot to deal with. I am responsible to love, to care, to counsel (when asked), to extend grace. But what someone does with that is his or her choice, his or her responsibility. I learned, by the way, that some people do not want to grow or change; they just want to be professional counselees.

Incidentally, when you think you are responsible for someone else's life and healing and they do not respond to your input, you become very frustrated and controlling. Their failure to heal, grow, or change affects how you view yourself, although it shouldn't. And no one likes a controlling person. I didn't have to be the fourth person of the godhead. That became a good mantra, reminder, and pressure reliever for me. I was not called to do things only God can do. I had almost destroyed myself with being so stinking responsible. You can totally wear yourself out trying to fix or help someone who doesn't even want to be fixed or helped. Brilliant!

Overly responsible or totally irresponsible, choose your dysfunction. Do you want your coffee too hot or too cold? How about just right? It is easier to get food just right than to get our thinking and our choices just right. It is the third part of the serenity prayer that is the hardest—wisdom to know what you can change and what you cannot.

> You can totally wear yourself out trying to fix or help someone who doesn't even want to be fixed or helped.

Many issues I could not fix; only God could. For a period of time, the pendulum seemed to swing the other way, and I no longer cared much about anyone else's issues. That, of course, is not God's answer, either. He extends grace, and we extend grace, but each person is responsible for his or her own growth in grace. With time, I trust I have become more balanced.

There were some who had been willing to be there for me, but I soon learned that most did not want to hear about the hard parts. *Let's just skip through to the victory* was the message I often received. I began to believe that if you laugh, the world laughs with you; but if you cry, you cry alone. That is not always true and is not true for everyone, but I chose my close confidants very carefully.

One time when I told a women's leader about one of our church's deeply hurting and damaged ladies who wanted to share her story, the leader said, "Oh, I don't want to hear it." My response was that we must and thus bear one another's burdens and so fulfill the law of love. Maybe we have a tendency to see pain and suffering and damage as a contagious disease we are afraid we will catch. A lot of people just don't want to hear it.

> Wallowing in our pain and enjoying our victimhood is a snare. Our failure and pain do not need to define who we are.

I do agree, however, that we need to process our grief and loss and then move on to victorious, life-giving faith and serving. Wallowing in our pain and enjoying our victimhood is a snare. Our failure and pain do not need to define who we are.

## Healing Scripture

Right after my painful discovery, I spent hours searching for a Scripture verse I could claim—one that, if I believed it, would guarantee that all this would turn out for good and not destruction for my children. I looked for months. I never found a verse that would give that guarantee. I found many promises I could claim for myself that would give me victory if I believed and obeyed. But there was nothing I could claim that would guarantee any particular outcome for others.

God is good, and He is powerful, but He has given people free will. He will not violate any individual's right to self-direction. We all have to choose what we will do with the trials of life, including the offenses and injuries we experience. I decided the best I could do for others was claim the promises for myself, do the work, be the best I could be, and say, "Come on in, the water is fine. Healing is possible, great things are ahead for you."

During the early days of my grief, various Scriptures sustained me. I read this passage over and over again. When I was especially low, I would tell my husband, let's read it again.

> *Oh, bless our God, you peoples!*
> *And make the voice of His praise to be heard,*
> *Who keeps our soul among the living,*
> *And does not allow our feet to be moved.*
> *For You, O God, have tested us;*
> *You have refined us as silver is refined.*
> *You brought us into the net;*
> *You laid affliction on our backs.*
> *You have caused men to ride over our heads;*
> *We went through fire and through water;*
> *But You brought us out to rich fulfillment.*
>
> —Psalm 66:8–12

Knowing that God was sovereign, in control, and especially that He was aware of what I was going through was soothing to my soul. And He is good. We went *through* not *into* the fire and water, but

## What I Have Learned

ultimately He has brought us out to rich fulfillment; one translation calls it *abundance*.

He has refined us *"as silver is refined"* (Zech. 13:9). Silver is put into a crucible and heated to remove the impurities. The refiner watches carefully and turns up the temperature just enough to remove the scum, the impurities that rise to the surface. The silversmith knows when the heat has done its work when he sees his own image in the silver. God desires our lives to be a reflection of Him, but for me, it took a lot of time in the crucible to remove the impurities. *Thank You, Lord. You still haven't given up on me.* That is what James means when he says to *"count it all joy when you fall into various trials"* (James 1:2). He doesn't say we are to feel joy but to "count" it as joy. Why? Because doing so works good things into us like patience, perseverance, and maturity.

Another source of joy and healing I had during those early years was my little granddaughter Alyssa. When I was having a blue day, Donnie would say, "I think you need an Alyssa fix." When we arrived to see her, she was so happy to see me, and it always buoyed my spirit. Once when we arrived, she ran around in circles with glee. Yes, she was my fix, my upper, and she still is.

Incidentally, my three daughters have all become beautiful women, inside and out, victorious and overcomers. I am so proud of them. The word *overcomer* implies there is something to overcome. The word *victorious* implies there have been battles, wars, and struggles. Do you expect to be a victorious overcomer? Know that you will have to fight battles to experience the victory of an overcomer.

The apostle Paul said, *"I have fought the good* fight, *I have finished the race, I have kept the faith"* (2 Tim. 4:7, emphasis added). Victory and overcoming is way more fun than sitting and stewing in our juices.

Paul also said, *"I press on, that I may lay hold of that for which Christ Jesus has also laid hold of me"* (Phil. 3:12). Can you see the picture? Paul is pressing onward, stretching upward to lay hold of the prize while Christ is laying hold of him to assist and ensure that he reaches God's goal for him. I love that image. So, with Paul, we can *"press toward the goal for the prize of the upward call of God in Christ Jesus"* (Phil. 3:14).

I knew I had to forgive. Forgiveness is not an option. The Bible is very clear that if we do not forgive others, our sins will not be forgiven; we will live in torment. I learned that forgiveness is a choice. It is not a feeling, nor is it an acquittal. Forgiveness does not mean saying, "It's okay, what was done is no big deal," when it is a huge deal.

But how do you forgive someone when you see no real repentance or remorse? It is especially hard when the one who hurt you is probably in denial about his guilt or the magnitude of the damage his behavior has caused. How do you forgive a person who minimizes, blame-shifts, rationalizes, and justifies his actions? I have learned that this is very typical of those who cause offense and harm. In fact, it is typical of all of us.

None of this, however, releases me of the responsibility to forgive. Very often, the offender begins to feel he is the victim—misunderstood and abused. I am quite sure the one who produced the hurt does not recognize the magnitude of the pain he caused me. Forgiveness has never been asked of me. Not a problem, though. I have totally forgiven and have prayed as Jesus did on the cross, *"Father, forgive them, for they do not know what they do"* (Luke 23:34). And they really do not. Forgiveness does not necessarily mean restoration of relationship and trust. Often, that is coinage that has already been spent.

I knew with the Lord's help I could forgive; and I did forgive. But what about the others? Could they forgive? Refusing to forgive is not only disobedience to the word, but it is to stay stuck, to live in bondage to the one who has hurt you. It has been said that the defilement of hatred, anger, and bitterness can be the price we pay for someone else's wrongs.

The apostle Peter warns us that we can be poisoned by bitterness. *"For I see that you are poisoned by bitterness and bound by iniquity"* (Acts 8:23). Hebrews 12:15 says that God wants to give us grace to forgive and warns us to beware, because just a little root of bitterness springing up can cause many to be defiled. Know for sure that bitterness and a lack of forgiveness are very defiling.

So forgiveness is absolutely not an option. Forgiveness breaks those chains and gives us freedom. It is a choice, a decision. Feelings will come and go. Live by your choices and your decisions, not by your feelings. Why should we allow the negatives in our lives and the wounds caused by others to dictate who we are? Let it go! Dump it into the ocean of God's forgiveness, and don't go fishing there!

> Why should we allow the negatives in our lives and the wounds caused by others to dictate who we are?

I also realize people can minimize the harmfulness of their behavior for so long that they believe their own rationalizations and fail to see the deep pain they have caused. According to Revelation 3:17, any of us can think we are doing great and not realize that we are "wretched, miserable, poor, blind, and naked" and thus deceive ourselves. Self-deception is pretty common. Offenders can do this, but so can the offended. We are not responsible for the offender's harm, of course, but we are responsible for any harm we cause.

Again, David said in Psalm 139:23–24, *"Search me, O God, and know my heart; try me, and know my anxieties; and see if there is any wicked way in me."* Then he adds, *"And lead me in the way everlasting."* We need help to see ourselves honestly. If we expect to receive grace, which we all so desperately need, then we must be willing to extend grace.

## Chapter Eighteen
## Let's Learn from Job

I had believed that if I trusted God and prayed and believed, nothing really tragic would happen to me. I was a little better than Job's counselors. I knew there would be hard times, but I basically believed the hard times would be only hard enough to build a little character. You know, just big enough to make a more interesting testimony. So I assumed—no, *believed*—that nothing really shattering would happen in my life, nothing so unthinkable that it could seem to write "Finished" across my heart and dreams. God could never allow anything like that to happen in my life, could He? Would He?

> I had believed that if I trusted God and prayed and believed, nothing really tragic would happen to me.

How is your story going? Is it all that you set out to make it? Has life met your expectations? Is it going the way you planned, the way you dreamed? What could break your heart may be very different from what could and did break mine. Heartbreak can come in many colors and shades.

In those times when tragedy and pain strike, when our hearts are broken and life doesn't make sense (we so want it to make sense, don't we?), we ask, *Where is God? Where is He?* And then we ask, *"Why?" Why? Why? Why?*

And next, we want to assign blame. (Like my dad when the car broke down—who failed to pay attention and take care of the details? Whose fault is this?) Either the devil caused this or God caused this, or this is entirely my fault and God is punishing me for my sins. The likelihood is this: the devil caused it, but God allowed it. After all, God is sovereign.

Please do not misunderstand me. I am not saying that God is the author of any evil thing. He is not. But He is the master of it. God is sovereign. He is the blessed controller of all things. To gain any benefit from a tragedy or a hurt, we must give it to Him. Only God can bring good out of bad. Only God can give *"beauty for ashes"* (Isa. 61:3).

Let's consider Job, God's servant. I do not want to claim that my suffering can compare with Job's great loss and pain. But God has given us the book of Job, and we can learn much from a study of his story. It became a focus for me in those days. If my pain, my loss, and my grief is not considered as great as others, that doesn't mean my anguish is not valid. It was my brokenness. It was very real to me.

> *Now there was a day when the sons of God came to present themselves before the LORD, and Satan also came among them. And the LORD said to Satan, "From where do you come?"*
> *So Satan answered the Lord and said, "From going to and fro on the earth, and from walking back and forth on it."*
> *Then the Lord said to Satan, "Have you considered My servant Job, that there is none like him on the earth, a blameless and upright man, one who fears God and shuns evil?"*
> *So Satan answered the LORD and said, "Does Job fear God for nothing? Have You not made a hedge around him, around his household,*

*and around all that he has on every side? You have blessed the work of his hands, and his possessions have increased in the land. But now, stretch out Your hand and touch all that he has, and he will surely curse You to Your face!"*

*And the* LORD *said to Satan, "Behold, all that he has is in your power; only do not lay a hand on his person."*

*So Satan went out from the presence of the* LORD.

*Again there was a day when the sons of God came to present themselves before the* LORD, *and Satan came also among them to present himself before the* LORD. *And the Lord said to Satan, "From where do you come?"*

*Satan answered the* LORD *and said, "From going to and fro on the earth, and from walking back and forth on it."*

*Then the* LORD *said to Satan, "Have you considered My servant Job, that there is none like him on the earth, a blameless and upright man, one who fears God and shuns evil? And still he holds fast to his integrity, although you incited Me against him, to destroy him without cause."*

*So Satan answered the* LORD *and said, "Skin for skin! Yes, all that a man has he will give for his life. But stretch out Your hand now, and touch his bone and his flesh, and he will surely curse You to Your face!"*

*And the* LORD *said to Satan, "Behold, he is in your hand, but spare his life."*

*So Satan went out from the presence of the* LORD, *and struck Job with painful boils from the sole of his foot to the crown of his head. And he took for himself a potsherd with which to scrape himself while he sat in the midst of the ashes.*

*Then his wife said to him, "Do you still hold fast to your integrity? Curse God and die!"*

*But he said to her, "You speak as one of the foolish women speaks. Shall we indeed accept good from God, and shall we not accept adversity?" In all this Job did not sin with his lips.*

—Job 1:6–12, 2:1–10

The conversation between the Lord and Satan in Job 1 and 2 is perhaps the strangest conversation in the Scriptures, or anywhere else for that matter. Satan had received permission from God to come against Job and everything he owned. All Job's sons and daughters and all his flocks and herds and servants died. Job said, *"Naked I came from my mother's womb, and naked shall I return there. The LORD gave, and the Lord has taken away; blessed be the name of the LORD"* (Job 1:21).

Then God allowed Satan to attack Job physically. Job did not blame God for these tragedies, nor did he rail against Him. But Job did recognize God's sovereignty. God is in control. We know that God declared from the outset that Job is *"a blameless and upright man, one who fears God and shuns evil"* (Job 1:8).

What was Satan's assessment of what Job would do? He believed he would curse God. To curse God means to renounce Him. That is what many so-called Christians do when tragic things happen. They say, *If this is what you are going to do in my life, I am not going to serve you anymore. In fact, I don't believe in You. You do not exist.*

Whom did Satan use to come against Job? First, he used Job's wife. She told him, *"Curse God and die!"* (Job 2:9). Some have been hard on Job's wife for not being more supportive of Job in his trial. But put yourself in her place. She, too, had lost everything, including all her children. Now she was watching her husband suffer.

God never comments again on Job's wife, and we shouldn't, either. She is not included at the end of Job's story when we are told God would not even hear the prayers of Job's friends. He said they must go to Job, offer burnt sacrifices, and ask him to pray for them, which he did after all their accusations and the torment they caused.

And remember Peter, who denied Jesus? He would become a leader of the early church, but Satan used him to come against Jesus when Jesus was saying He must suffer and die. Jesus said, *"Get behind Me, Satan!"* (Matt. 16:23). Jesus recognized the source.

## Let's Learn from Job

When Job's friends came around and saw his suffering, they threw dust on their heads and sat in silence for seven days, which was appropriate. And then his friends began tormenting him with various accusations. What had happened to him was entirely his fault, they said. It was sin in his life. God never allows tragedy into the life of one who is living a life of integrity, they reasoned.

Great friends! This kind of torment is worst of all. To be told that all the destruction and pain your loved ones have experienced is all your fault is excruciating. And usually, we do not need friends to tell us that. Those thoughts can already be in our minds, especially if we have a faulty concept of God like Job's friends had. We reason, *Be good and you will be blessed; be bad or sinful and you will be blasted.*

That pretty much makes us sovereign, doesn't it? It puts us in control of our destiny. *Tragedy has come, and it must be the consequence of sin in my life.* That was the conviction of Job's friends. They included God in their assessments, but they put these simplistic parameters around Him. Remember, God was not pleased with Job's friends. Beware of putting God in a box by declaring you know more of His ways than are knowable.

Again, we do not need friends to tell us this. Why are those thoughts so easily in our minds? Because we are all sinners. We have sinned and made mistakes. *It must be sin in my life that has brought this catastrophe on me.* These thoughts are not our friends. These self-condemnations are not productive and only exacerbate our pain. Were it not for God's compassion and mercy, I know I would be toast. But isn't that true of all of us?

> Beware of putting God in a box by declaring you know more of His ways than are knowable.

It's interesting how just a small misconception about God can cause us to come to some very misguided conclusions. A ship that's off a mere degree will eventually go way off course. So beware of jumping to the conclusion that God is out to get you or anyone else because of sin and failure.

We speak of the patience of Job. I felt rather guilty when I wanted to escape, to die. I recognize that my tragedy was nothing compared to Job's. Job is called a man of great patience, yet he certainly asked why. And even though he was not suicidal, he longed for death. He cursed the day of his birth (Job 3:1). He wanted to know why God didn't let him just die. *"My soul chooses strangling and death rather than my body"* (Job 7:15). *"Why then have You brought me out of the womb? Oh, that I had perished and no eye had seen me. I would have been as though I had not been. I would have been carried from the womb to the grave"* (Job 10:18–19).

After reading of Job's longing for death, I felt a little less ashamed. When we are hurting, we want to escape the pain. I was not suicidal but simply wished I could go to sleep and not wake up. That is not pretty, but it is a natural human response.

And Job wanted to know why these things had happened to him. Sixteen times Job asks why. He wanted to make sense of his ordeal. Somehow, when I saw this in Job's story, I related and was comforted. I wanted to know why, and I wanted to make sense of things.

So what do we learn from Job's story? First, did God know what Job was going through? Yes! He absolutely knew. He allowed it to happen for reasons that were God's alone to know. Throughout Job's suffering, God never abandoned him for a minute. Job felt abandoned, but he argued for God's sovereignty throughout, and at the end, he said, *"I know that You can do everything, And that no purpose of Yours can be withheld from You"* (Job 42:2). God is sovereign. Job never gave Satan credit or blame. He never spoke of the fiery darts of Satan, but he did speak of the *"arrows of the Almighty"* (Job 6:4).

If we belong to the Lord, we need to remember that when we find ourselves in painful circumstances or feeling broken (1) God knows; (2) God cares; (3) He sees the beginning and the end; and (4) He has a future and a hope for us. So if God is aware (and He is), and if God loves us (and He does), and if God is sovereign and the blessed controller of all things (and He is), how are we to make sense of what is happening when we suffer?

You may be saying with me, *I am not Job. And I don't want to be Job. God has a Job. He doesn't need another one.* None of us volunteers to go through pain, suffering, grief, and loss. Guess what? It is not a case of volunteering. Bad stuff happens to everyone. As Forrest Gump said, "My momma always said, 'Life was like a box of chocolates. You never know what you're gonna get.'"[1]

What did Job know that his friends did not know? He knew that there was more to God, more to what God was doing, than the simple boundaries his friends were putting around Him. You cannot put God in a box. We should never assume we know or can predict exactly what God is doing or is going to do.

Do you suppose God is insulted when we treat Him like a heathen god we can manipulate and control? Rub the Buddha's tummy, and he will bless you. Job said that we only know *"the mere edges of His ways"* (Job 26:14).

I love that. God in His great love and compassion and wisdom has chosen to reveal a great deal about Himself to us. It is His desire that we know Him. John 1:18 says, *"The only begotten Son, who is in the bosom of the Father, He has declared Him."* The New International Version reads, *"has made him known."* We know Him through His son, through creation, and through Scripture. And yet ultimately, we know *"the mere edges of His ways."*

I am suspect of the prosperity gospel, that if you give to God, He will give back to you health, wealth, and prosperity. I don't believe that if we have enough faith, we will never be sick or suffer want. I think of the hall of faith individuals in Hebrews 11. The first 35 verses describe great triumphs of faith, but the last five verses record the courageous faith of many who suffered great torture, torment, and even death, refusing deliverance. The writer of Hebrews says of them, *"the world was not worthy"* (Heb. 11:38). No, we only know *"the mere edges of His ways."*

I know a couple that was deeply wounded by being told their baby would not have died if they had had enough faith. That means the death was their fault. How dare some sanctimonious, so-called Christian make such a statement? It sounds like Job's counselors, doesn't it? Yes, great blessings come from loving and serving the Lord, but the Scriptures warn us and prepare us for suffering, also. Our refining seems to require some trials. We are to *"count it all joy"* (James 1:2).

And Job wanted to have it out with God. He almost demanded an audience with God. *"I would speak to the Almighty, and I desire to reason with God"* (Job 13:3). The Living Bible translation puts it this way, *"Oh how I long to speak directly to the Almighty. I want to talk this over with God himself. Yes, I will take my life in my hand and say what I really think. God may kill me for saying this—in fact, I expect him to. Nevertheless, I am going to argue my case with him"* (Job 13:3, 14–15 TLB). Wow! That is pretty bold. Job wanted to know what he did wrong and why God allowed this devastation to come into his life.

After all of Job's struggle, cursing the day he was born and arguing with his friends, God showed up. Might this be called searching for God with all your heart? Note that God did *not* give Job the answer to the questions he was asking—why did this happen? What did I do wrong?

What did happen? God gave Job an exam. God had some questions for him. *"Then the LORD answered Job out of the whirlwind,* and said, *'Who is this who darkens counsel by words without knowledge? Now prepare yourself like a man; I will question you, and you shall answer Me'"* (Job 38:1–3). Then God proceeded to question Job. *"Where were you when I laid the foundations of the earth? Do you know the time when the wild mountain goats bear young? Can you draw out Leviathan with a hook? Have the gates of death been revealed to you?"* (Job 38:4, 38:17, 39:1, 41:1). For 105 verses, from Job 38–41, God questions Job. He asks him more than 70 questions about creation. Who hung the stars in space? Who made the crocodile? Who set the boundaries of the sea? And on and on.

How does this relate to Job's suffering? What does creation have to do with Job's turmoil? It almost seems as though God were mocking Job. What was God's point?

God was shifting Job's focus. If we cannot understand creation, what makes us think we can understand the ways of the creator? Some have said that if we can't even understand the common house cat, what makes us think we can understand God? We are astonished by the complexity of the eyeball, not to mention the one who made it. Only in recent years have we begun to unravel some of the mysteries of DNA. God is God. We are not.

What was Job's response? He was awestruck. His breath was taken away. It shut his mouth. Twice Job put his hand over his mouth. And he repented.

That is what anyone will do when they come into the presence of the living God. When Peter recognized the deity of Jesus after the huge catch of fish at Jesus's command, he said, *"Depart from me, for I am a sinful man"* (Luke 5:8).

The Lord then told Job's three friends to go to Job, offer burnt offerings, and ask Job to pray for them. God's wrath was aroused against them because they had not spoken *"what is right, as My servant Job has"* (Job 42:7).

Here is what is interesting. *"The LORD restored Job's losses when he prayed for his friends"* (Job 42:10). They had been humbled, and Job was gracious. Obviously, Job forgave them for the torment they had caused him.

Job didn't see what God allows us to see. At the beginning of the story, God draws back the curtain just a little and allows us to see the scene between Him and Satan. We see that God is, indeed, sovereign. We see that we have an enemy, but God is in control and Satan can go no further and do no more than God allows. A bigger drama is taking place in the universe, in the heavens, and Job is given a part to play—a much bigger part than I would guess he wanted to play.

But I still have a hard time getting it. Why would God allow Job, a man He declared was righteous and blameless, to go through all this pain and loss just to prove some point to Satan? *"Have you considered My servant Job?"* (Job 1:8) It's almost as though God is pointing Job out to Satan to go after him.

As I have pondered this question, I have come to believe God was not allowing this to prove anything to Satan but to show us something. God was actually setting Satan up, not Job. All along, I believe God was using Satan for His own purposes, for Job's ultimate good, and for our learning. And Satan fell for it.

In the end, God's sovereignty was established. His glory, power, wisdom, and love were shown, and Job was restored, blessed, honored, and approved. A refining process had occurred. We hear no more about Satan. Satan can do his best, but God is God over all, including Satan. Wow!

## Benefits of a Job-Like Experience

Job went through a lot, but he did eventually have an astounding encounter with Almighty God. He came to know God in a more personal way. He said, *"I have heard of You by the hearing of the ear,*

## Let's Learn from Job

*but now my eye sees You. Therefore I abhor myself, and repent in dust and ashes"* (Job 42:5–6). Can you imagine the terror, the wonder, and awe of such an encounter with God Almighty? Job was unquestionably never the same. God is all about our relationship with Him, and that is where Job experienced a breakthrough.

The apostle Paul said that it was worth the loss of all things *"that I may know Him"* (Phil. 3:10). God desires that we know Him.

*Thus says the LORD:*
*"Let not the wise man glory [boast] in his wisdom,*
*Let not the mighty man glory in his might,*
*Nor let the rich man glory in his riches;*
*But let him who glories glory in this,*
*That he understands and knows Me,*
*That I am the LORD, exercising lovingkindness, judgment, and righteousness in the earth,*
*For in these I delight," says the LORD.*

—Jeremiah 9:23–24

Yes, Job came to know God more profoundly. Could God have stopped Satan from bringing so much devastation into Job's life? Of course He could have, but He didn't. And He had His reasons for allowing Job to suffer the losses he did.

### I Will Never Doubt God's Love

When we go through devastation and heartbreak, we often ask these questions: *Does God really have a big heart? Does He really love me? Does He ever just toy with us?* When excruciating pain and hurt come, we are tempted to think three things: (1) He doesn't know; (2) He doesn't care; or (3) He isn't big enough to do anything about it. None of that is true. If you are His child, He does know, He does care, and He is in control and beyond powerful.

There is a lot I did not understand about what God was doing in my life. As Job said, we know *"only the edges of His ways."* But one thing I know is this: God loves me. He loves *me*! God is love. I feel like a preschooler with crayons as I struggle to capture and display God's love and grace.

I am ashamed to admit there was a time when I did not like myself, so I wondered how God could love me. Then one day I had a vision of Him with His arms spread wide, the crown of thorns on His head, and blood running down as He hung on that cross. I heard Him saying, *What more must I do to demonstrate my love to you, Carol?* I was shamed and saddened by how much my doubt must have hurt His heart. I purposed to never again question His love for me.

John refers to *"that disciple whom Jesus loved"* (John 21:7). He says in another place, *"Now there was leaning on Jesus' bosom one of His disciples, whom Jesus loved"* (John 13:23). Although the disciple "whom Jesus loved" is never named in Scripture, the tradition of the early church designates him as John, the author of the book of John. I figured Jesus didn't love John more than the others. The little word *more* is what hangs us up. If John was referring to himself, I don't believe he was saying he was loved more than others. He simply knew Jesus loved him.

So I have decided to call myself "that woman whom Jesus loves." I am perfectly content if you decide to call yourself the same thing. In fact, I would be delighted. Jesus is love. There is plenty to go around. His loving you does not diminish His love for me. It is His love that enables us to love one another. Amazing! My heart's desire is to be known as one who loves.

When someone loves you only for what he or she can get out of you, is that love? No, of course not. But that is the way many of us love, and that's how we sometimes think of God. We have created a God out of our own imaginations. *I will trust you as long as you bless me, but if you don't, I am through with you. You don't exist to me.*

That is not love, and it certainly is not faith. When my mom heard about my heartbreak, she was afraid I would lose my faith and turn back on my walk with the Lord. No, I did not lose faith; I lost heart. My cry was, "No way, Lord, I am not turning back. I may be the worst player on the team, but You are stuck with me. You will have to see me through this trial. I don't like this, I don't understand how this could have happened, but I am Yours and You are stuck with me." End of statement! Besides, where else could I go? As the disciple Peter said, *"Lord, to whom shall we go? You have the words of eternal life"* (John 6:68).

## Tried Faith

So we have trials and disappointments. Our faith gets tested. Hebrews 11:6 says, *"Without faith it is impossible to please Him."* Untried faith is not real faith. First, Peter tells us that trials prove the genuineness of our faith, and that such faith is *"much more precious than gold that perishes, though it is tested by fire, may be found to praise, honor, and glory at the revelation of Jesus Christ"* (1 Peter 1:7). Tested faith is precious to God.

I related to Job in two areas. I maintained with Job: *"Though He slay me, yet will I trust Him"* (Job 13:15). I was hanging on for dear life. *I am not doing too well here, Lord, but I am hanging on*, I told Him. Do you suppose Job is disappointed in the role he played in the drama of the ages? He is and will be for all eternity a trophy of God's grace.

And second, I felt like Job in that *"the thing I greatly feared has come upon me"* (Job 3:25). Could that be a warning about fear? I have pondered that question a great deal. Could fear about something actually attract the fulfillment of that fear? Someone has said there are 365 *fear nots* in the Bible. It is a common issue with us to be fearful, so God has given us a *fear not* for every day of the year.

Is living in overpowering fear evidence of a lack of faith? He has not *"given us a spirit of fear, but of power and of love and of a sound mind"* (2 Tim. 1:7). Without God's grace, I could not have survived but would have continued to shrink back in faithless fear, shame, and devastation. Want joy in the midst of pain? I believe the Scriptures teach us that the more suffering, pain, and hurt we experience while still maintaining our faith in the love and hope of Christ, the greater opportunity we have to become a trophy of God's grace for all eternity.

Paul said in Romans 8:18, *"For I consider that the sufferings of this present time are not worthy to be compared with the glory which shall be revealed in us."* I am ashamed of my whining. I have suffered so little compared to so many others. It is easy to scold myself 30 years after I first discovered the devastation, but at the time, I was in overwhelming shock and grief. Still, my goal is to respond to the grace given me and trust Him to make me one of His *"trees of righteousness, the planting of the LORD, that He may be glorified"* (Isa. 61:3)—a trophy of His grace, kindness, and healing.

## Another Story More Powerful than Job's

I am glad the story of Job is in the Bible. It reveals some important truths about God. But I am thankful that Job is not the only revelation of God that we have. In Job, God gave man an audience. But in the Gospels, God became a man. He humbled Himself to enter into the story.

In a novel or a drama, we usually don't get acquainted with the author. He or she is behind the scenes, omniscient and in control of the events. We identify with the characters in the story. Through the incarnation, God came into the story. He became a man, a human being. Now we can relate to Him as one of us.

And what part does God play in this drama? He is the pursuer. He is the lover of our souls. He is the rescuer. I am not the hero of the story—He is. But I am the object of His love. I am the beloved. We think we pursue God, but Romans 3:11 says, *"There is none who seeks after God."* He pursues us. God became a man and dwelt among us. He came as a servant and humbled Himself to the point of death, even the death of the cross. Why? He came to purchase us back to Himself, to redeem us because He loves us. He is the hero of our story, our prince. The book of Revelation actually portrays Him at one point coming on a white horse. Amazing drama of the ages!

First John 4:10 says, *"In this is love, not that we loved God, but that He loved us and sent His Son to be the propitiation [sacrifice, acceptable payment] for our sins."* God is staking everything on the proposition that love is more creative and more powerful than manipulation or force. He has taken the great risk of giving people a free will. By doing so, He has in some ways chosen to limit Himself.

He does not force people to love and obey Him. He could have made us little robots, but then where would love be? Without choice, there is no possibility of love. Do you want a person to marry you because he or she has no other choice? If there's no choice, no danger, no risk, then there's also no love.

# Chapter Nineteen
# Do Not Give Up Your Dreams

It has become a dream, a goal, and a burden of my heart to minister healing and comfort to those who have found themselves in deep pain and depression. The source of the pain and depression is as varied as there are variations of people. Many times, however, parents find themselves in profound grief, sorrow, and confusion because of the mistreatment or choices of their children. Much is available and written for the relief of the children, but not so much for the parents. Where do we go for help? Are there support groups for our help, programs for our healing and restoration?

My dream is to be a source of encouragement, a source of hope and comfort for all who experience devastation in their families or any form of devastation. Life can go on. The sun can come up again. Life can have meaning for us. We can have fulfilled dreams. I write to you who have experienced pain, grief, and loss of any kind. Perhaps your sorrow is not exactly the same as mine, but if you are grieving from failure, shame, hurt, betrayal, or disappointment, my dream is to share the encouragement I have found in the Lord.

Is your disappointment and sorrow the result of a hurt your loved ones have experienced? Or have you fallen down yourself? Regardless of the source of your pain, you must get up. You cannot give up. Do you know the difference between a slip and a fall? A slip is when you stumble and go down, but you get back up. A fall is when you go down, stay down, give up, and refuse to get up. That is a fall, a failure. Don't be a quitter.

## Wilma Rudolph

A person who never gave up was Wilma Rudolph. Born into poverty in the racially segregated South and weighing 4.5 pounds, she was the 20th of 22 children in her family. She overcame pneumonia, scarlet fever, and childhood polio, which she contracted at the age of four. The polio weakened her left foot and leg requiring her to wear a brace and then orthopedic shoes until she was eight. Because she lived in a town with no medical care available for blacks, she and her mother bussed 50 miles for two years for medical treatment and therapy at Meharry Medical College. She also received messages (treatments) from her family at home, provided four times a day.

She overcame her debilitating disabilities by the time she was 12, and by high school, she excelled in basketball and track. Although disqualified in the preliminaries for the 100-meter race, she and her team won the bronze in the 4x100 relay in the Melbourne, Australia, Olympics in 1956 when she was only 16. Back home, she told her classmates that she was going to win gold in the next Olympics. Don't you love it? She set her goal, she verbalized it publicly, and she claimed the victory beforehand.

She competed in the 100-meter, 200-meter, and 4x100 relays in the 1960 Olympics in Rome, Italy. She won three gold medals, the first American female to do so. Rudolph is remembered as a world-record-holding champion and an international sports icon in track and field. They proclaimed her the fastest woman in the world in the 1960s. Following her success, she became an advocate for civil rights for many years. Her role model was Jesse Owens from the 1936 Olympics.

Rudolph said, "Never underestimate the power of dreams and the influence of the human spirit. We are all the same in this notion:

The potential for greatness lives within each of us."[1] So don't be a quitter; don't give up on your dreams.

And please, oh please, do not believe the lies of the enemy. If you have had what you consider a significant failure in your past, the liar will whisper, *You are hopeless; you are no good; you are a failure; you will never amount to anything. You are a lost cause, even to the Lord. None of your dreams will ever come to fulfillment.*

We rehearse these lies in our minds until we believe them; they become our truth. We fail to recognize the source of the lies, so we believe them. Proverbs 23:7 tells us, *"For as he thinks in his heart, so is he."* That is a powerful truth. What are you saying in your heart to yourself? What is your self-talk? You talk to yourself in ways you would never speak to a friend. You become your own worst enemy. Be careful what you say to yourself. Are you a negative person about yourself and others? The truth is that you must decide whom you are going to believe, Jesus and His word or the liar. Warning: these lies you believe are straight from the pit. Are you believing Satan and calling Jesus a liar? Be very careful that you're not believing lies.

> You talk to yourself in ways you would never speak to a friend. You become your own worst enemy. Be careful what you say to yourself.

Jesus says you have tremendous worth. You are a treasured, prized, valued human being. How valuable are you? He says He would rather die than live without you. He would not die for trash. He died for your forgiveness so you can be a new creature in Christ, renewed day by day. When you receive Him as your Lord and Savior, God calls you His child, a child of the king. That is pretty heady stuff, a child of a king, of *the* king. That makes you a prince or princess.

When you invite Christ to come into your life, His cleansing blood washes your heart white as snow. You were a sinner, but you died with Him in baptism, you were buried with Him, and you came up out of that death to newness of life, His Spirit in you. Wow! What good news! You are as pure as a bride prepared in purity for your groom. Unfathomable but true!

We can do all things *"through Christ who strengthens [us]"* (Phil. 4:13). He says, His *"strength is made perfect in weakness"* (2 Corinthians 12:9). Read Scripture, meditate on it, rehearse the truth, and speak it out loud. When we hear truth out loud coming from our own lips, we begin to believe it.

When we rehearse our worthlessness or hopelessness, we believe it, even though it is a lie. Be careful what you say. I try to rehearse this to myself: "I am strong; I am capable; I am funny; I am a winner; I am victorious; I am loved; I am forgiven; I am a child of the king; I am an overcomer; I am growing in His grace; I am successful; I am being renewed every day. I am not the great I AM, but through His grace, I am what I am, and I am what He says I am." Hallelujah! Excuse me while I dance a jig.

I started to write this book several years ago. I believed the prompting to write had come from the Lord, that His amazing presence and power in our lives must be recorded for the next generation. We are commissioned to pass the baton to those who come after us. But I got to the hard part, and I quit. How could I write of the heartbreaking tragedy and shame that had come into my story? Maybe others involved were not ready for their stories to be documented.

But I knew I could not write of all the victories and miracles as though I were someone who never had to go through times of severe pain and heartbreak. I was not an icon of strength and virtue without major weaknesses and failures. Was it even wise to come out of the shadows and share all the failure and shame, especially when it involved others?

For over a year I stopped writing. I just quit. In March 2017, I was challenged to pick up my dream of writing this book. My heart and my vision are to be used to proclaim healing, comfort, consolation, and hope to others with broken hearts and shattered dreams. Someone out there—perhaps you—needs to know that God is longing to give you *"beauty for ashes, the oil of joy for mourning, the garment of praise for the spirit of heaviness"* (Isa. 61:3).

In the book of Genesis, Abraham's father, Terah, is an example of a person who failed to go on, to finish strong. Genesis 11:31–32 tells us that Terah took Abram to go out *"from Ur of the Chaldeans to go to the land of Canaan; and they came to Haran and dwelt there. So the days of Terah were two hundred and five years, and Terah died in Haran."*

He started to go to the land of Canaan but stopped in Haran. He stopped short; he didn't go on to Canaan. We are not told why he stopped. Maybe it was too hard. Maybe he was tired. Maybe he got comfortable in Haran. Maybe he lost the vision, the dream, to go to Canaan. But the point is that he stopped. *"So the days of Terah were two hundred and five years, and Terah died in Haran"* (Gen. 11:32).

All kinds of stumbling blocks and discouragements can dissuade us from continuing with our dreams and goals. Often, these distractions are not reasons; they are excuses. I do not want to go halfway. I do not want to give up on my dreams. I do not want to be a Terah, a quitter. I do not want to live without a vision, to be dead while I live, to live my life without passion for the Lord.

Babe Ruth said, "You just can't beat the person who never gives up."[2] My prayer for you is that you begin to see the power in having dreams. Don't give up on your dreams. Don't let heartbreak or loss stop you from having dreams and goals. Dream big, and believe that God will bring those dreams, desires, and visions to fulfillment. The Bible says that without a vision, the people perish. Lots of people are still living, but they've died inside. God wants us to live with passion. I believe He wants us to dream big dreams and see those dreams fulfilled for His glory.

We give up on our dreams too easily. A devastating thing happens, and we hang it up. We give up. We figure we are finished. But our God is the God of second chances—second and third and fourth chances. Sometimes, we get tired, or we get busy with our lives and stop imagining any dreams at all. We just settle for existing, merely surviving.

Don't you hate the idea of merely settling? I don't want to settle for less than what God has for me. It's kind of like New Year's resolutions. Even when we write them down, we rarely revisit them. By the next year, we are in the same place as the previous year and don't even remember what we set out to do.

A New Year's resolution is not the same as having a burning desire for something. When we have an overwhelming, burning desire for something, we go for it. It is constantly on our minds. By God's grace, it *will* happen.

We need to visualize those dreams coming true. Write them down in a vision book or on a vision board. Pray and praise God—every day—as though they have already happened. I am learning that this is the practice of all successful people.

Faith is seeing those things that are not as though they are. Let me say that again. Faith is seeing (visualizing) those things that are not as though they are. That comes straight from the Bible. Tell Him you only want His will for your life, and then go for it. The enemy (we have one, you know) would like to stop us right there with doubts about where our dreams come from, thoughts that our dreams are not His. *Oh, I don't know if this dream, this vision, is from God. Maybe it's just something I want. Maybe it is pride. How can I think such things could ever happen for me?* Or our enemy reminds us that we have failed in the past, so why do we think we can accomplish anything now? Don't believe those lies.

> Faith is seeing those things that are not as though they are.

If Jesus is Lord of your life, your heart's desires are more than likely from Him. He said in John 15:7, *"If you abide in Me, and My words abide in you, you will ask what you desire, and it shall be done for you."* If the dream is bigger than you are or is too much for you, that's good. Now you are getting into God-sized, God-honoring prayers and dreams, the kind that showcase His glory. Write them down—in detail. Revisit and rehearse them every day.

If you have a dream, you must decide if it is a pipe dream, a wish, or a God-given, driving purpose and challenge meant for you to pursue. Again, I tell you, to really change your life, your dream must become a burning desire, an obsession in your heart, an almost do-or-die passion. It is said that David *"sat before the LORD"* (2 Sam. 7:18). Take time to sit quietly before the Lord. Is there a desire, a dream you've had, something you believe He has placed on your heart?

We ought to pursue what we truly desire—that which sets our hearts on fire. Then we must begin taking the necessary action to make it a reality. Begin taking little, doable steps. Ask God for the next step.

Sometimes our passion will come from our broken hearts, our shattered hopes. I did not want to waste my pain. I believe God did not want to waste my pain. The hurt is lessened—mitigated—when we find a redemptive purpose for it that gives meaning to our heartbreak.

I almost gave up on finding any purpose or a meaningful outcome to my broken heart. I would simply go on, live the Christian life as fruitfully and maturely as I could, and try to forget my heart. Revisiting my brokenness was rarely enjoyable. Could I ever imagine a way God could use my broken heart for His glory? Is this my platform to declare His grace, His presence, and His purpose in my small life?

Actually, I am amazed at the many incredible dreams and visions the Lord has fulfilled in my life. Psalm 37:4–5 says, *"Delight yourself also in the LORD, and He shall give you the desires of your heart. Commit your way to the LORD, trust also in Him, and He shall bring it to pass."* I learned early on that this verse did not mean God intends to give us our every little whim or want. When God gives us our desires, it means they are His desires. *"He shall give you the desires of your heart"* (Ps. 37:4). He will place the desires in your heart. Then He loves to bring them to fulfillment.

By the way, if you want to know the secret to delighting yourself in the Lord, go to Isaiah 58:13–14. That is another passage the Lord showed me very early in my walk with Him, even before Donnie became a believer.

> *If you turn away your foot from the Sabbath,*
> *From doing your pleasure on My holy day,*
> *And call the Sabbath a delight,*
> *The holy day of the LORD honorable,*
> *And shall honor Him, not doing your own ways,*
> *Nor finding your own pleasure,*

*Nor speaking your own words,*
*Then you shall delight yourself in the LORD;*
*And I will cause you to ride on the high hills of the earth,*
*And feed you with the heritage of Jacob your father.*
*The mouth of the LORD has spoken.*

I found that Scripture after my recommitment while going through our old white family Bible. Over the years, when Donnie and I went on mission trips, teaching cruises, or other places, we got to do some amazing things, go to some amazing places, and meet some amazing people. I would wonder, *Lord, is this what you meant by riding on the high hills of the earth?* When some of my dreams were fulfilled, I would ask that question again. Is this what Isaiah 58 means?

Some people who call themselves Christians seem to see little obligation to be faithful to church attendance. I know this is not popular teaching today, but Hebrews 10:25 reads: *"not forsaking the assembling of ourselves together, as is the manner of some, but exhorting one another, and so much the more as you see the Day approaching."* Do you suppose the Lord expects obedience to that? I know churches are not perfect and many who attend are not even true believers (the Bible calls them tares, not wheat), but that doesn't mean going to church is optional or unimportant.

Complaining about hypocrites in the church is just an excuse. You wouldn't throw away all $20 bills just because there are some counterfeit 20s out there, would you? Seventy years ago, when I was growing up, going to church was what Christians did on Sunday mornings. In fact, all the stores and businesses except a few bars were closed on Sundays. (That really dates me, doesn't it?) Sunday was simply considered the Lord's day. How can we claim to love the Lord and not love his body, His bride?

My mom became a believer about the time I did. With her help, we were always faithful to attend Sunday school, morning church, evening church, and Wednesday-night prayer meeting. When I was old enough to attend youth fellowship, she made sure I was there. When I was older and complained it was boring, she said, "Well, you get in there and make it not boring." No excuses.

They gave out little pins for perfect attendance in Sunday school. I had a pin for a year of perfect attendance and at least five little hanging additions on my pin signifying five more years of perfect attendance. If we went on a vacation, which we almost never did, we would find a church so I would not break my record of perfect attendance. So later, I knew how to claim the promises of Isaiah 58.

I'm thankful to dear Mom because she taught me faithfulness to the Lord based on commitment, not feelings. That brand of commitment is so missing today. I guess I am old-fashioned enough to believe that if we want to know God's will for our lives, we need to obey what is already clearly shown in Scripture as His will. We need to find a God-honoring, Bible-teaching church and then go and support it.

## Chapter Twenty
## Finding Our Joy in the Lord

So how do we go about finding our joy in the Lord? The Scriptures give many insights into how to do this. Keep in mind that feelings are not necessarily right or wrong; they just are. We cannot reach up and turn off sad feelings like switching off a light. But feelings can be used to awaken us to our wrong thinking. When we are depressed and sad, we need to check our thinking. What thoughts are circling round and round in our minds? What are we saying to ourselves?

It is our thinking that drives our feelings, and we do have control over how and what we think. If the Bible tells us to bring every thought captive to the obedience of Christ, it must mean that with His help we can do it. It may be difficult, but we can and must confront our thinking and reprogram our beliefs to line up with God's word. We need to search the Scriptures to find the lies in our thinking. Proverbs 23:7 says, *"For as he thinks in his heart, so is he."* Thinking about the truths of Scripture gives hope and is a salve for our wounded souls. Rehearsing the negative lies of the enemy leads to depression and hopelessness and death. It is a choice.

What are some of the lies we tend to believe? If we are Christians, and especially if we are pastors' wives, we think we are supposed to be perfect, always above reproach. Furthermore, if we fall short, we have not just messed up; we are failures.

Is this biblical? No, it is not. *"If we confess our sins, He is faithful and just to forgive us our sins and to cleanse us from all unrighteousness. If we say that we have not sinned, we make Him a liar, and His word is not in us"* (1 John 1:9–10). So if we sin, we deal with it before the Lord and go on. The lie is to believe we are failures, that we are hopeless, and that God is done with us—that He will not continue to forgive us. He tells us to forgive 70 times seven. Will He do less? Remember, failure is when we give up, when we don't get back up and keep walking with the Lord.

We tend to believe that we need the approval of everyone, especially our peers or close circle. That is not always possible, and it is not true. We can expend untold energy seeking the approval of others. Not everyone is going to support and appreciate everything about us. If we believe we cannot be okay without the endorsement of everyone in our circle, we are setting ourselves up for colossal disappointment and loss of joy.

Tragically, another lie we believe is that our dreams and desires will never be fulfilled. We begin to think that what we have to offer has no value or worth, that life has passed us by and that it is too late to pursue the desires of our heart. We totally lose heart. The enemy loves it when we believe that one.

This past week was very challenging for me. I had had the flu for two weeks during and after a family reunion in Alaska. I had finally recovered, and at the end of another trip to Texas for my new husband's class reunion, I came down with another bout of flu. All of this happened in about four weeks. I was sick, tired, and thinking maybe I was supposed to give up. Maybe God was not in this endeavor after all.

Then just this week, the Lord gave me two specific encouraging words. The first encouragement came from 2 Chronicles 15:7: *"But as for you, be strong and do not give up, for your work will be rewarded"* (NIV). Isn't that delightful? I came upon that verse just when I needed an encouraging word from the Lord.

And the second came from 2 Corinthians 9:8: *"And God is able to make all grace abound toward you, that you, always having all sufficiency in all things, may have an abundance for every good work."* For some reason, this one was very hard to memorize. I like to memorize Scripture to rehearse as I go to sleep. Note the three *all*s and encouraging words like *abound, always, sufficiency,* and *abundance.* And also note that it says that *"God is able"* to bring these things about. I dare not give up.

I must mention, however, that this verse is in the midst of Paul's teaching about giving. I think this passage is addressed to those who are generous, sacrificial, and cheerful givers. (Context, context, context. How is your giving to the Lord going?)

## Manifold Grace for Manifold Trials

*"My brethren, count it all joy when you fall into various trials, knowing that the testing of your faith produces patience [endurance]. But let patience have its perfect work, that you may be perfect and complete, lacking nothing"* (James 1:2–4). James says *count* it all joy. He didn't say *feel* it all joy.

Another verse uses that word *various*. *"As each one has received a gift, minister it to one another, as good stewards of the manifold grace of God"* (1 Pet. 4:10). The word *various* and the word *manifold* are the same Greek word: various trials and various graces. They could be translated *many-colored*. Many-colored grace for many-colored trials. The Lord is telling you that for every trial, there is a matching grace. When a fellow Christian is going through manifold trials, we are to minister to him or her with the manifold grace of God.

Think of an outfit you like to wear. You want the colors to match. So when you go through a trial, God is telling you He has a matching grace that perfectly matches that trial. Cool, right? Easy to say, but when you are hurting, it's not so easy to believe. Nevertheless, it is true.

What is grace? Primarily, grace is God doing in your life what you cannot do and what you do not deserve. It is His enabling. It is not something you can earn; it is freely given. And, oh, how badly we need His grace when we are going through painful losses and grief, when the trials of our lives can tempt us toward despair.

> Grace is God doing in your life what you cannot do and what you do not deserve.

To whom does God give this enabling grace? *"God resists the proud, but gives grace to the humble"* (James 4:6). The answer is to the humble.

When we are going through a trial, we must not say, *I don't deserve this.* Instead of asking, *Why me?* we should ask, *Why not me?* We must change our thinking. It is not all about us.

During testing, we ought not imagine we are better than others, either. It's no time for arrogance and pride. When we are going through tough times, we certainly cannot afford to have God *resist* us. That is scary. It's tough to have anyone resist us, but to have God resist us? That's a terrifying thought. And James says, *"God resists the proud."*

Twice the New Testament tells us, *"God resists the proud, but gives grace to the humble"* (James 4:6; 1 Pet. 5:5). These verses echo Proverbs 3:34: *"Surely He scorns the scornful, but gives grace to the humble."* Likewise, Isaiah 57:15 says, *"I dwell in the high and holy place, with him who has a contrite and humble spirit."* So the call for humility is not a minor command or concept. It was because of pride that Satan was cast out of heaven.

I found this Scripture to be a good checkpoint in my early years as a wife and mother. Have you ever felt like you were losing it? You were upset, frustrated, or just plain mad at someone? You wanted to scream or hit something or somebody? The situation was not fair! Right? When I found myself in that losing-it mode, I learned to stop and think. God would like to grant me grace for this situation, but I obviously was not experiencing His grace.

My pride was the problem. Ultimately, I always found that self had been ruling my spirit. I had been entertaining thoughts like these: *I deserve better than this. Why doesn't he or she see what he or she is doing to me? I am just going to look out for me for a change.* Stopping and humbling myself beneath the mighty hand of God and crying out for His presence and strength would result in my peace being restored. Yes, God resists the proud but gives grace to the humble.

It always worked when I was willing to stop, reflect, and surrender. But to be honest, it required some growing on my part and the willingness to quickly relinquish enjoying my pouting and my personal pity party. Have you ever been there?

We need God's grace when we are drowning. I knew His grace was my only lifeline. And the Scriptures say to humble yourself. Again, like joy, humility is a choice. Humility involves recognizing that God is sovereign, that He is in control, and that He is good. It involves bowing before Him concerning the disappointments in our lives.

We need to know and believe the truth that trials are sent for our transformation and maturity and as opportunities for God's glory. Like James 1:2 says, we count trials joy because they produce results in our lives.

# Chapter Twenty-One
# Right Thinking about Joy

Our feelings are neither right nor wrong, but they can give us powerful insight into our thinking and can indicate where our thinking is off. If we have stinking thinking then we will have stinking feelings and no happiness.

Joy and happiness are not the same. Happiness comes from the word *happenstance*, and what happens is somewhat *hap*hazard.

Hap means chance. Happiness is external. Joy is internal. Happiness is based on circumstances. Joy is based on Christ. Happiness is based on chance. Joy is a choice.

Joy requires that we discipline our thinking. Happiness is always out of our control. It is simply based on the haphazard happenings in our lives—the weather, other people's choices, our health, the money in the bank (or lack thereof), or the pizza we ate last night.

Here is a powerful verse telling us where to direct our thinking:

*Finally, brethren, whatever things are true, whatever things are noble, whatever things are just, whatever things are pure, whatever things are lovely, whatever things are of good report, if there is any virtue and if there is anything praiseworthy—meditate on these things.*

—Philippians 4:8

And how do we do this? The previous verses illuminate the process:

*Be anxious for nothing, but in everything by prayer and supplication, with thanksgiving, let your requests be made known to God; and the* peace of God, *which surpasses all understanding, will guard your hearts and* minds *through Christ Jesus* (emphasis added).

—Philippians 4:6–7

Notice that verse eight refers to meditation, thinking, and your mind—not your feelings. When you are in the throes of pain and disappointment, being immersed in your feelings is understandable and human. Eventually, however, to experience healing, overcoming and victory will require disciplined thinking.

Do you realize that Paul was bound in chains in Rome when he wrote those verses? Yet he rejoiced and counsels us to rejoice, too. Why did he rejoice? He rejoiced because God was working maturity into his life and using him to further the gospel.

Great joy is experienced in serving and trusting the Lord and in remembering that this life is but a breath, a vapor. Paul said that for him to live is Christ and to die is gain. Why could he say to die is gain? It was because Paul's focus was on eternity, on heaven, not on the temporal, the here and now. We will consider more of that perspective later.

Horatio Spafford composed the words of the song "It Is Well with My Soul" at a time of overwhelming tragedy. His wife and children had perished when a ship they were on went down in the Atlantic. He returned to the place where the ship sank and composed the moving lyrics below. I doubt these words were based on feelings or happiness or circumstances, but rather on a choice to trust God.

## Right Thinking about Joy

When peace, like a river, attendeth my way,
When sorrows like sea billows roll;
Whatever my lot, Thou hast taught me to say,
It is well, it is well with my soul.

*Refrain:*
It is well with my soul,
It is well, it is well with my soul.

Though Satan should buffet, though trials should come,
Let this blest assurance control,
That Christ hath regarded my helpless estate,
And hath shed His own blood for my soul.

And, Lord, haste the day when my faith shall be sight,
The clouds be rolled back as a scroll;
The trump shall resound, and the Lord shall descend,
Even so, it is well with my soul.

Why was it well with his soul? Spafford's thoughts went to the time when his faith would become sight in eternity at the return of Christ for the redeemed.

## Chapter Twenty-Two
## Choices We Must Make

Other choices must be made if you are going to experience joy. There are certain things you could call killjoys. These are things you will have to give up if you are going to know joy.

You will have to give up that hurtful past. If you don't give up your past, it will ruin your present, and you will have no future. Good advice. Listen to the apostle Paul on the need to forget the past:

*Not that I have already attained, or am already perfected; but I press on.... Brethren, I do not count myself to have apprehended; but one thing I do, forgetting those things which are behind and reaching forward to those things which are ahead. I press toward the goal for the prize of the upward call of God in Christ Jesus. Therefore let us, as many as are mature, have this mind; and if in anything you think otherwise, God will reveal even this to you.*

—Philippians 3:12–15

Paul acknowledged that he hadn't reached his goal yet, but that he was moving toward it. He didn't look back; he pressed on. And I love that God is involved in enabling us to have the right mind, the right thinking. When we are offtrack, He is faithful to reveal that to us. "If in anything you think otherwise, God will reveal even this to you." Wow! That's good news! I am slow in my thinking, but God faithfully corrects me. What a God!

## Joy Killers

So here are some keys to letting go of the past and moving on to joy. We must get rid of the killjoys and turn them over to God.

### *Grudges*

You must give up your grudges.

> *Get rid of all bitterness, rage and anger, brawling and slander, along with every form of malice. Be kind and compassionate to one another, forgiving each other, just as in Christ God forgave you.*
>
> —Ephesians 4:31–32 NIV

Note that it says we are to *"get rid of"* these things. We are to forgive as God has forgiven us. We must give up our grudges. It says to throw them away. If you have been hurt in the past, deeply hurt, the temptation is to grow bitter and stay that way. Bitterness is a poison you drink in the vain hope of making someone else sick. Will bitterness change the past? No, but it *will* destroy the present.

*"Looking carefully . . . lest any root of bitterness springing up cause trouble, and by this many become defiled"* (Heb. 12:15). Bitterness will not touch the person who hurt you, but it will defile all your present relationships and damage those people you love, the ones you love the most. Note that it requires only a "root" of bitterness, a grudge you refuse to release.

The Living Bible puts Hebrews 12:15 this way: *"Watch out that no bitterness takes root among you, for as it springs up it causes deep trouble, hurting many in their spiritual lives."*

*But he/she/it makes me so angry.* No one can make you mad or bitter without your permission. Don't let the past control you. Let it go. You can't run away from it, either. It just goes with you. And it will damage all future relationships because bitterness impacts you and everything you touch.

*"Beloved, do not avenge yourselves, but rather give place to wrath; for it is written, 'Vengeance is Mine, I will repay,' says the Lord"* (Rom. 12:19). Give your anger, your hurt, to God. He can handle it. If vengeance is appropriate, God will handle it the right way at the right time.

> I must deal with my own wrongs and leave judgment of others to God.

First Peter 2:23 says that when Jesus *"was reviled, [He] did not revile in return; when He suffered, He did not threaten, but committed Himself to Him who judges righteously."* That verse always stops me in my tracks. God judges righteously. I have my side of the issue; the person who offended me has his or her side. Again, God judges righteously. Might I be due for judgment, also? Famous TV host Dr. Phil says that no matter how flat you make a pancake, there are always two sides. I must deal with my own wrongs and leave judgment of others to God.

## Grief

You will also need to give up your grief. Sorrow and grieving is a normal part of life in this present world. Everyone experiences loss. It hurts. Isaiah says of Jesus that He was *"a Man of sorrows and acquainted with grief"* (Isa. 53:3). Jesus said, *"Blessed are those who mourn, for they shall be comforted"* (Matt. 5:4). *"Jesus wept"* (John 11:35) when he was at the grave of Lazarus. Paul tells us that we have sorrow, but not as those who have no hope (1 Thess. 4:13).

Yes, you will encounter painful, hurtful things in this life. Everyone processes his or her grief in his own way and for different lengths of time. We are wise not to press those who are suffering loss to rush through their time of grief.

But it is possible to hang on to your grief until it turns to self-pity. When you live in self-pity, you resign from life. You are no good to yourself or anyone else. Some wallow in their grief and almost enjoy the attention, finding pleasure in being a victim.

David had to deal with grief after he was told that his and Bathsheba's baby would die. Scripture tells us that he grieved and pleaded with God and would not eat for six days. When the baby died on the seventh day, the servants were afraid to tell David. When the child was still alive, he would not listen to them or be comforted, and now that the child had died, they were afraid he would do some harm.

When David perceived that the child had died, we are told that he rose from the ground, washed and anointed himself, changed his clothes, and went into the house of the Lord and worshiped. He transformed his grief into a focus on God through worship. Then he went home and ate. He accepted the fact that the baby had died, and he bowed to God's sovereignty. God had spoken, and he would accept it.

Change a situation if you can, but when you cannot, accept it. Amy Carmichael (1867–1951), an amazing missionary to India, often said in her writings, "In Acceptance lieth peace."[1] I have counseled myself with her wise statement numerous times. Quit fighting the things that cannot be changed. With acceptance comes peace.

Sounds a lot like the serenity prayer, doesn't it? "God, grant me the serenity to accept the things I cannot change, the courage to change the things I can, and wisdom to know the difference."[2] We simply can't change some things. I could not change the fact that heartbreaking events had occurred in the past. I had to accept it. But I needed the wisdom to know if and how it could be used in my life and in the lives of others.

Focus and perspective are vitally important. We must focus on what we do have, not on what we have lost. David focused on God in worship. God is God and we are not.

A college girl wrote a letter to her parents that went something like this:

Dear Mom and Dad,

I am sorry I haven't written. I have been very busy and I have met a man. He is 20 years older than I but we have fallen in love, and I have moved in with him. We are now engaged. He is very kind. I am sure you will love him too. He is looking for better work, but since he has little education, it has been difficult. He is of a different nationality and religion, but we get along very well. I know you have always wanted grandchildren, so you will be thrilled when I tell you I am pregnant. Because of the pregnancy, I have dropped out of school.

Love,
Your daughter

P.S. None of the above is true, but I wanted you to have the right perspective when I tell you that I am getting a C in Econ 101 and need more money.

Yes, perspective is vital. The greatest impact on our thinking is when we see the events in our lives from the perspective of eternity. Will what is happening in our life matter for eternity? Will it matter next year? Next week? An eternal focus impacts everything. Belief in heaven is a tenant Christians adhere to, but it seems to have minimal influence on the way we live in the here and now.

> The greatest impact on our thinking is when we see the events in our lives from the perspective of eternity.

*Guilt*

And you will have to give up your guilt. Staying stuck in overwhelming feelings of guilt will certainly rob you of joy. We have all sinned. We say, *I know God has forgiven me, but I just can't forgive myself.* That kind of thinking sounds humble and repentant, but actually it is arrogant. Are you so much more holy than God that He can forgive you but you cannot forgive yourself? No, it is not that you can't; it is that you won't.

Which raises this question: What gives us the right to forgive ourselves? Where do we get the liberty, the permission, and the gall to let ourselves off the hook? It is the cross that gives us permission to forgive ourselves. Without the cleansing blood of Christ, there would be no basis for forgiveness for anyone.

Jesus died for my forgiveness, and to refuse to forgive myself is to say that His blood was not sufficient. I confess and repent, and forgiveness is granted on the basis of His sacrifice, not on my worthiness.

I am not saying that it is always easy, especially when our sinful acts have done great harm. Nor am I saying that we should take sin lightly. If restitution is required or possible, then we should make restitution.

Some people hang on to their guilt with the mistaken idea that it is humility, that they are serving God by punishing themselves and showing how sorry they are. Wallowing in guilt and sitting on the sidelines of life is not what God's forgiveness is about. Such thinking is wrong. The good news is that God forgives. He may have to forgive over and over as we struggle with habits and besetting sins, but He gives grace for forgiveness and for growth and for overcoming as we cry out to Him.

There is a right way and a wrong way to deal with guilt. Both Judas and Peter denied Jesus just before He was crucified. Judas became hopeless and committed suicide. Peter was despondent, but he was repentant, ultimately accepted forgiveness, and was used mightily by God.

We can deal with guilt in at least four ways. We can *repress* it. That is, we can try to push it down until we are no longer aware of it. It exists only in our subconscious, we'd like to think.

We can *suppress* it. That is a conscious effort to keep it secret, to refrain from disclosing or divulging the wrongs we have done. That doesn't work, either.

We can *express* it by doing more of the same, by continuing to act out. We say, *Hey, everybody, look at me. See what a lousy person I am. I'm hopeless, I can never change.*

Or we can *confess* it. We agree with God about our sin. That is what it means to confess. *Con* means *with*, and *fess* means *to say, to speak*. We agree and say with God that something is sin; we quit calling it something else. We quit justifying it, and we stop rationalizing and making excuses for it. And we don't blame others.

We don't beg God to forgive us. He wants to forgive us more than we want to be forgiven. He died for our forgiveness. Nor do we bargain with God. *God, if you forgive me this one time, I promise I won't ever do it again.* (That is a promise we can sometimes keep and sometimes not.)

*God, if you forgive me, I will give 20 percent of my income, or I will be a missionary.* No, we don't beg God. We don't bargain with God, and we don't blame others for what we have done. We own it.

> We don't beg God to forgive us. He wants to forgive us more than we want to be forgiven.

So we must let go of our grudges (the people who have hurt us). We must let go of our grief (the things that are out of our control). And we must let go of our guilt (the things we have done that have hurt others.)

*Fear*
Many are in bondage to fear. Fear is another joy killer. A discussion of anxiety disorders and irrational fear is beyond the scope of this book, but debilitating fears, including extreme nervousness and irrational thoughts, are very common in our culture. It has been suggested that such disorders are America's number-one mental health problem, costing billions in medical bills and workplace losses. Many names are used to differentiate between the disorders—panic disorder or panic attacks; post-traumatic stress disorder (PTSD); social phobias; and now a new designation, generalized anxiety disorder (GAD).

Some people suffer from relatively insignificant, illogical fears, while others are afflicted with more serious and seemingly bizarre phobias. The range of disorders has become quite expansive and can rarely be justified or even understood. The source of these fears is the mind—beliefs held in the mind and in our thinking. Fear does not produce courage. To be courageous, fear must be overcome enough to allow for action.

Not being a particularly fearful person, I am reluctant to make any simplistic pronouncements concerning fear and those who suffer debilitating anxiety disorders. I actually have such a phobia about snakes, even totally harmless snakes. I sometimes experience an irrational physical response to a sudden picture of a snake on television, not to mention happening upon one outside.

Once, when traveling to Indonesia on a mission trip, our host at a brief stopover in Biak offered to take us to see a Japanese cave used during World War II. We were transported on the back of his flatbed truck through some tall grass and weeds. Then we stopped, and everyone else hopped off to follow him down into the cave.

I almost didn't go. A cave? Surrounded by tall grass? But I didn't want to wait on the back of the truck, so I jumped down and caught up to the rest of them. Sure enough, someone ahead of me said, "Oh, look at the red snake up on those branches." Oh, great! Snakes!

I remember immediately thinking, *God did not bring me all this way to kill me or to terrify me with a stupid little red snake.*

I can testify that for the rest of the trip and for some time after, I noticed that my phobia was much abated. I can't explain it, but I believe it was changing my thinking that eased my fears. I focused on the Lord. I had chosen to act in spite of my phobia, thinking about my fear more rationally. The result was that it became less threatening. I learned that I could often talk myself out of freaking out at the sight of a snake, which is a little embarrassing when the snake is only on TV.

So I'm not going to say that all you have to do is trust Jesus and you won't have any fears. That would be simplistic, naïve, and arrogant. I do believe, however, that trusting in the presence of Christ and His enabling grace can alleviate a great deal of our fears in general and can give us the courage to act in spite of the fear we feel.

Remember? There are apparently 365 *fear nots* in Scripture. That tells me that God is aware of our tendency to fear, and His prescription is to recognize His power, presence, and enabling in every situation. So fear and worry and anxiety are joy stealers. Work to see your fears in light of the Lord's promises.

## *Griping*

Another joy killer is griping. Have you ever been around people who gripe, gripe, and gripe? They can even depress us and annoy the joy out of any situation. Did you know that focusing on what you don't have actually attracts more of the same? When we voice our complaints and gripe about our situations, we create the environment for more of the same.

If you complain about being poor, you will stay poor. If you whine about being unloved, you will not attract love. If you grumble about your life never changing or improving, your situation will stay the same. Complain about always being in debt, and you will stay in debt, or it might even get worse. No, griping does not produce joy nor does it produce the power for change, growth, or improvement.

What is the antidote for complaining? Gratefulness! If you want to change your life and your situation, you must quit voicing your gripes and begin speaking gratefulness. Life and success coaches all agree that to attract positive things in your life, you must voice thankfulness for the good things you do have. That attitude will actually attract more good things and events and success.

> *Be anxious for nothing, but in everything by prayer and supplication, with thanksgiving, let your requests be made known to God; and the peace of God, which surpasses all understanding, will guard your hearts and minds through Christ Jesus.*
>
> —Philippians 4:6–7

Gratefulness expresses itself to others, but especially to God. Give God thanks for all the blessings in your life. There's good advice in a line of the little song "Count Your Blessings": "Count your many blessings, name them one by one."[3] How long has it been since you have made a list of all God's blessings in your life?

Psalm 103 is a chapter I have committed to memory. *"Bless the LORD, O my soul; and all that is within me, bless His holy name! Bless the LORD, O my soul, and forget not all His benefits"* (Ps. 103:1–2). We can get into the habit of forgetting His blessings. David goes on to itemize the many blessings of the Lord on his life. I have found that this chapter is a good source of meditation at night when I am struggling to fall asleep.

The apostle Paul wrote, "In everything give thanks, for this is the will of God in Christ Jesus for you" (1 Thess. 5:18). Gratefulness is not only a good practice to attract even better results, but it is a command that we need to obey. Gratefulness is God's will for us. Why would we search to know God's will for our lives when we are not obedient to what has already been revealed as His will?

It does not say we must be grateful *for* everything, but *in* everything. Some things are not good in themselves, but when we give thanks in those times, God can enter into the situation and turn them around for our good and for His glory. Can you believe that? In His power, sovereignty, and love, He actually turns painful, difficult events and circumstances into blessings. Believe it! Thank Him for it and then watch for it.

Again, the apostle Paul tells us in Romans, *"And we know that all things work together for good to those who love God, to those who are the called according to His purpose"* (Rom. 8:28). My husband used to tell his people that he looked up the meaning of the little word *all*, and guess what? It means *all*. It does not say that all things look good or feel good at the time, but that God is working all of them together for good. The greater good, of course, is that we might be conformed more into the image of Christ, that we might become more like Jesus.

It is amazingly powerful to thank God for our desires that have not yet been manifested. That demonstrates faith that pleases God. He has planted His desires into our hearts. Now thank Him for the fulfillment of those dreams before they are accomplished. Don't doubt! Worship! *"Now faith is the substance of things hoped for, the evidence of things not seen"* (Heb. 11:1).

I believe, by faith, in the seemingly impossible completion of this book. I am thanking God that it will not only be completed but that it will bring healing, release from bondage, beauty for ashes, and the oil of joy for mourning, *"that they may be called trees of righteousness, the planting of the LORD, that He may be glorified"* (Isa. 61:3).

The King James Bible says in Psalm 22:3 that God inhabits the praises of His people. People are the inhabitants of their homes. To inhabit something means to dwell in it, so we can conclude that God dwells in the praises of His people. If you want to attract God's presence in your life, praise Him.

He does not abide in your gripes, whining, and negativity. God hates complaining and sees it as unbelief. It was because of complaining that God condemned the Israelites to ultimately wander in the wilderness until all those over 20 years old died there. They thought they were complaining against Moses, but they were really griping against God. Scary but true; He hates complaining.

> God hates complaining and sees it as unbelief.

They asked over and over why He brought them into the desert to die. Weren't there enough graves in Egypt? Here is a terrifying verse: *"Say to them, 'As I live,' says the LORD, 'just as you have spoken in My hearing, so I will do to you: The carcasses of you who have com-*

*plained against Me shall fall in this wilderness . . . from twenty years old and above'"* (Num. 14:28–29).

Listen to yourself. What are you expressing, voicing? Get excited about your future and the things God wants to do in your life. Start thanking Him now.

Yes, we must deal with our grudges, our grief, our guilt, our griping, and our fears (I couldn't think of a "g" word for fears). But joy involves more than what we must give up. There are also things we must embrace.

# Chapter Twenty-Three
# Right Thinking about Pleasure

Let me make some comments and observations about pleasure. We learn from Scripture that there is pleasure in sin for a season. We are told that those who live in sin are dead while they live. We call them hedonists, people who live only for pleasure.

We know the story of the prodigal son is about a man who spent all he had seeking pleasure. The fun lasted until the money ran out, and then he ended up in a pigpen wanting to eat husks.

The problem was, not that he sought pleasure, but his thinking that the best pleasures could be experienced as far away from his father as he could get. We are told he went to the far country. The irony is that when he repented and came home, there was acceptance and a big party. He was looking for pleasure in the wrong places.

But is pleasure in itself evil? Pleasure is a great motivator. Much money, time, and effort are expended in the pursuit of pleasure. Here are some verses about pleasure.

- Psalm 16:11: *"You will show me the path of life; in Your presence is fullness of joy; at your right hand are pleasures forevermore."*
- Psalm 147:11: *"The Lord takes pleasure in those who fear Him, in those who hope in His mercy."*

- Ephesians 1:5–6: *"Having predestined us to adoption as sons by Jesus Christ to Himself, according to the good pleasure of His will, to the praise of the glory of His grace, by which He made us accepted in the Beloved."*
- Ephesians 1:9: *"Having made known to us the mystery of His will, according to His good pleasure which He purposed in Himself."*
- 2 Thessalonians 1:11–12: *"Therefore we also pray always for you that our God would count you worthy of this calling, and fulfill all the good pleasure of His goodness and the work of faith with power, that the name of our Lord Jesus Christ may be glorified in you, and you in Him, according to the grace of our God and the Lord Jesus Christ."*

These and other Scriptures speak of God's pleasure and of His taking pleasure in us. Since God finds pleasure, we know that pleasure in itself is not sinful. So much of His pleasure is in blessing us. That is not only amazing but also pretty exciting.

Consider Psalm 35:27: *"Let the LORD be magnified, who has pleasure in the prosperity of His servant."* So the Lord finds pleasure in our prosperity. I believe He wants us to prosper not only spiritually but also financially. It is so easy to assume that a desire to be financially comfortable is not spiritual. Where do we get those ideas? We make our gracious God into some kind of hard-hearted, calloused ogre. If you think this way about God, you are serving a God not revealed in the Bible. Yes, He disciplines us when He must, but it is because He loves us. He doesn't take pleasure in it.

## God Finds Pleasure in Giving

Let's examine Luke 12:32 more closely. *"Do not fear, little flock, for it is the Father's good pleasure to give you the kingdom."* Jesus refers to us as His little flock. We are His sheep; He is our shepherd. All that

## Right Thinking about Pleasure

the shepherd is to us is outlined in Psalm 23. He keeps us from want. He prepares a table for our refreshment and strength. He gives us peace and rest in green pastures and beside quiet waters. He guides us to righteousness, and He is with us when we walk through the valley of the shadow of death. He never leaves us. And, of course, our good shepherd is none other than Jesus, who lays down His life for His sheep (John 10:11).

We read that it is the Father's good pleasure to give us the kingdom. Many of us have not had fathers who found great pleasure in giving to us. My father was not cruel; he was simply absent most of my life. It took me some years to realize I had hung that trait on my heavenly Father.

I knew Dad loved me because Mom told me so. I knew God loved me because the Bible told me so. But I thought of God as big, important, and busy—off somewhere too busy for me and not present or particularly mindful of me, just like Dad. I have finally grasped the truth that God is with me, my good shepherd, and very attentive to everything about me, even more so than when the sparrow falls. Yes, He is big beyond comprehension, yet He hears me when I cry out to Him. He is my Father. (I want to get up and dance a little jig.) He is my Father! Wow!

Where does this father find not just pleasure but good pleasure? *"It is your Father's good pleasure to give"* (Luke 12:32). He loves to give. That is His joy. It is His pleasure to generously provide for His children. He delights in giving without any strings attached. He is not stingy, and He's not looking to get paid back. He is king, and we are children of the king. It is His desire to give us the kingdom. I think we have very little conception of what the kingdom entails. In God's kingdom is a gracious, wise, loving, benevolent king.

And He recognizes our bent toward fearfulness, so He councils us with *"do not fear,"* even though we are *"little."* Why? Because He is our loving heavenly Father. So we should take great comfort when we read, *"Do not fear, little flock, for it is your Father's good pleasure to give you the kingdom"* (Luke 12:32). What a God!

I used to say to my kids as they left for school, "Remember whose kids you are." They knew I was not referring to me but to God. Fear and misbehaving are less apt to occur when we remember whose kids we are.

God desires to give us the kingdom, to give us life and not death, to give us abundance and not want, to give us the waters of life that satisfy us. The only qualification for His giving is that we thirst.

> *"Ho! Everyone who thirsts,*
> *Come to the waters;*
> *And you who have no money,*
> *Come, buy and eat.*
> *Yes, come, buy wine and milk*
> *Without money and without price.*
> *Why do you spend money for what is not bread,*
> *And your wages for what does not satisfy?*
> *Listen carefully to Me, and eat what is good,*
> *And let your soul delight itself in abundance.*
> *Incline your ear, and come to Me.*
> *Hear, and your soul shall live;*
> *And I will make an everlasting covenant with you—*
> *The sure mercies of David."*
>
> —Isaiah 55:1–3

For what are we thirsting? Are we hungering and thirsting for God Himself? Am I seeking Him with all my heart? Even after disciplining Israel, God still counseled them, saying, *"And you will seek Me and find Me, when you search for Me with all your heart"* (Jer. 29:13).

Psalm 16:11 is especially pertinent to our discussion about finding joy and pleasure in God. *"You will show me the path of life; In your presence is fullness of joy; At Your right hand are pleasures forevermore."* God shows us the way to Him, the ultimate source of joy and pleasure.

The word *beatitude* means supreme blessedness, happiness, or bliss. The Beatitudes, found in Jesus's Sermon on the Mount (Matt. 5:3–12), all start with the word *blessed*. My soul has clung for years to the fourth beatitude, *"Blessed are those who hunger and thirst after righteousness, for they shall be filled"* (Matt. 5:6). I know that I am not righteous. But it does not say, "blessed are the righteous." It says blessed are those who *"hunger and thirst for righteousness."* In that blessing I have staked my hope and my trust, believing that because I do hunger and thirst, I *"shall be filled."*

## Be a Giver

My precious mother found pleasure in giving, especially to her three kids. She was extremely frugal and seemed to enjoy saving every penny she could. She and Dad never lived lavishly, but Mom was especially careful and prudent with money. After Dad died, she had limited funds that she could have hoarded.

But she decided that since she had some insurance policies she could cash in, if needed, she would give some cash to us and enjoy the blessing of giving while she still could. One year, she gave each of us three kids $10,000. She said it would be more valuable to help meet our needs at that time rather than after she died when it wasn't worth as much. She was always mindful of the best value. The next year, she gave each of us kids and our spouses another $10,000, a total of $60,000. I think she enjoyed it more than we did, and Mom was not a terribly rich lady.

Do we think God enjoys our prosperity any less than parents delight to see their children do well? I don't think so. Guess what? Mom's generosity has inspired me to do the same. And it's great fun! And now my new husband has been motivated to do the same for his four boys.

Can love and giving flow more readily from a heart that has been broken? I believe it can and often does. It really is more blessed to give than to receive. Watch for little ways to give, to pay it forward, and you will experience amazing joy.

## Pursue the Lord, Not Happiness

Could our difficulty in finding joy, pleasure, and happiness result from the fact that we are not told to seek those things? Might joy and pleasure be by-products of something else, something different we are to seek or pursue?

The Declaration of Independence includes the well-known line: "All men are created equal, that they are endowed by their Creator with certain unalienable Rights, that among these are Life, Liberty and the *pursuit* of Happiness"[1] (emphasis added). It declares that we have the right to pursue happiness.

But Scripture does not tell us to pursue joy, pleasure, or happiness as ends in themselves. We are counseled to pursue God and His will, and that will result in joy and pleasure. Matthew 6:33 says, "Seek first the kingdom of God and His righteousness, and all these things shall be added to you."

David said *"As the deer pants for the water brooks, so pants my soul for You, O God"* (Ps. 42:1). He longed for the Lord Himself, not just for His gifts.

We are to *"pursue love"* (1 Cor. 14:1). We are told to *"always pursue what is good both for yourselves and for all"* (1 Thess. 5:15). And we read about pursuing godly relationships: *"Pursue peace with all people, and holiness, without which no one will see the Lord"* (Heb. 12:14).

Might the implication be that our supreme joy is found in learning to live, to walk, to have our existence and delight and joy in the pursuit of God and His ways?

We hear of people who seem to have everything—wealth, fame, success—all that the heart could desire. And yet they commit suicide. Why is that? What happens inside their hearts that causes such despair?

George Bernard Shaw once wrote, "There are two tragedies in life. One is not to get your heart's desire. The other is to get it."[2] Heads you lose, tails you lose. That's pretty pessimistic. Pursuing goals that do not include God and failing to pursue that for which we were created results in emptiness and despair. It is like striving for years to climb the ladder of success and then finding it was propped up against the wrong wall. Here is a better, more reliable path to success:

> *"This Book of the Law shall not depart from your mouth, but you shall meditate in it day and night, that you may observe to do according to all that is written in it. For then you will make your way prosperous, and then you will have* good success" (emphasis added).
>
> —Joshua 1:8

Not all success is good success. For one thing, good success is success without regret. This good success is not temporal; it is eternal. But why is it such a struggle to keep our focus on the eternal?

It's not that temporal blessings are bad. Money is not evil. It is the *love* of money that becomes a problem. Jesus spoke in Matthew of the many legitimate needs we have. His council is to *"Seek first the kingdom of God and His righteousness, and all these things shall be added to you"* (Matt. 6:33). The problem is not the many temporal attractions we desire in the here and now. The problem occurs when we allow legitimate temporal needs to become our primary focus. So we need to ask ourselves what we're seeking first and make sure it's God.

## Chapter Twenty-Four
## Finding Joy and Beauty in Serving Others

*"The Spirit of the Lord God is upon Me,*
*Because the Lord has anointed Me*
*To preach good tidings to the poor;*
*He has sent Me to heal the brokenhearted,*
*To proclaim liberty to the captives,*
*And the opening of the prison to those who are bound;*
*To proclaim the acceptable year of the Lord,*
*And the day of vengeance of our God,*
*To comfort all who mourn,*
*To console those who mourn in Zion*
*To give them* beauty for ashes,
*The* oil of joy for mourning,
*The* garment of praise for the spirit of heaviness;
*That they may be called trees of righteousness,*
*The planting of the* LORD, *that He may be glorified."*

*Instead of your shame you shall have double honor.*
*"Their descendants shall be known among the Gentiles,*
*And their offspring among the people.*
*All who see them shall acknowledge them,*
*That they are the posterity whom the* LORD *has blessed"* (emphasis added).

—Isaiah 61:1–3,7,9

## From Plowing to Preaching

I know that Isaiah 61 is a prophecy about Jesus. He is the one who is anointed to preach good news to the poor. He is the one who will break the chains that bind us. He is the comforter and consoler for all who mourn and the only one who can give beauty for ashes. Yet I believe this Scripture has been given to me as an assignment, a challenge in Him to share my story with the intent that others with unspeakable heartbreak and pain can relate and find comfort in an otherwise devastating time.

In Jesus, we are united through pain and can be a relieving balm of grace to others, a place of refuge for the hurting, and a light of hope for those who long for healing, joy, and a heart of praise. If we will but believe Him, He will make us *"trees of righteousness, the planting of the Lord, that He may be glorified"* (Isa. 61:3). It is not all about us. It is certainly not all about me. It is all about Him, that He may be glorified. I declare to you that as I have realized this more and more, my joy and praise and hope have grown exponentially. I have been freed to see His purposes, His vision, and His hope for my future.

Scripture declares that this life is but a vapor, a breath. Eternity is everlasting, forever. Let's give Him our days, our devastation, and our all and see what He will do with them. We want to give Him our gifts and abilities. But we need to give him our nothingness and emptiness, too. Remember, God is the one who can make something out of nothing. He spoke, and creation came into existence. We must remember His creative, renewing power when we deeply feel our nothingness.

Just because I was broken and damaged doesn't mean I should never be real and honest about the failures and the shame I sometimes feel. Jesus is a safe hiding place. Sometimes we find it comforting to just stay in that secret place with Him, never reaching out to bring healing to others. We don't have to stay in hiding, shrinking back from who He has made us to be. Isaiah 61:7 reads, *"Instead of your shame you shall have double honor."* It is a stunning verse and a liberating promise for me. Even with loads of shame and failure in our pasts, through Him we can experience honor—even *double* honor.

The word concerning our descendants, our offspring, and our posterity in Isaiah 61:9 gave me resounding encouragement. Could I expect that blessings would flow to my children as I surrendered to the stunning miracle of becoming a tree of righteousness, *"the planting of the LORD, that He may be glorified"* (Isa. 61:3)? I claim that as a word of hope from the Lord.

We are more than our past failures. We must not allow our past to dictate who we are in the present or ruin our future. I realize that is a nice-sounding admonition, but it can be tough to apply when we are talking about our own hearts.

We speak of the heart in so many ways. When we want someone to care, we say they should have a heart. When someone is unkind and unfeeling, we say they are heartless or have no heart. When we want to talk seriously to someone, we say we need to have a heart-to-heart talk. When someone is giving and caring, we say they are big-hearted. When someone is especially wicked, we say they have a black heart. When someone experiences deep hurt, we fear they will lose heart.

What about my broken heart? I have often recalled, *"Keep you heart with all diligence, for out of it spring the issues of life"* (Prov. 4:23). Could I risk baring my soul, my heart? Could I risk the anxiety of my broken heart being fully exposed and allow God to use my hurt and healing for the healing of others who need this fellowship of the brokenhearted? Hurt and rejection may come, but I have decided that the hurt of hiding and disappearing is worse. No matter what motivates us to hide, it is a lonely place. The decision to come out of hiding is one only I could make. Yes, I spent a month in a hospital in the psych ward. What kind of Christian victory and testimony is that?

## You Can't Buy Beauty in a Bottle

What does *"beauty for ashes"* mean in Isaiah 61? If your heart has been broken, you understand the *"ashes"* part. Something has been burned and destroyed, and only ashes remain. If you've suffered great loss, you understand what the *"mourn"* means in that passage. And you're familiar with *"the spirit of heaviness."* But how do we understand the *"beauty"* it talks about? Ask any girl, any woman, and if she is honest, she will confess that she wants to be beautiful. Little girls want to be pretty. My momma used to tell me, "Pretty is as pretty does." (That ranked right up there with "your eyes are bigger than your belly.")

What is beauty, anyway? Is beauty what big business tells us it is? Companies want to sell us their stuff. They know most women long to be beautiful. They show us the "beautiful" airbrushed people in their commercials and advertisements to convince us that if we just buy their hair spray, their boots, their car, their hemorrhoid ointment, we, too, will be beautiful. (I am amazed at all the ways "beautiful" is used to sell.) If we eat what they sell or buy their supplements and pills, we can be beautiful, shapely, and even skinny. We almost begin to believe the lie, and we buy, try, and buy some more.

Unfortunately, their definition and packaging of what is beautiful changes every season. The marketing gurus want us to continue to desire and continue to buy, so they go to great lengths to dream up new products and new advertisements along with new definitions and descriptions of what is beautiful.

But real beauty cannot be bought. It does not come in a bottle. That is shallow beauty, fake beauty, fraudulent beauty. We are disappointed and feel defrauded because we do not look like the people in the ads. But we continue to buy stuff, trying in vain to reach the elusive state of beauty we long for.

Have you noticed that almost every magazine you see as you go through the checkout line advertises a weight loss article? I wonder why. Someone knows that a huge percentage of us want to find the foolproof and painless answer to weight loss. Those articles sell. But there is no easy, foolproof, painless path to weight loss. I wish! How do I know? I think I have tried them all. There is no program where you can eat everything you want and still lose weight in a healthy way.

I am not suggesting that diligent care of our outward, physical appearance is unimportant. It is not unspiritual to make every effort to be as attractive as possible. We should do all we can to enhance our physical, outward appearance and honor our God-given bodies. Certain Christian cultures seem to suggest that being frumpy and dowdy is spiritual. Don't you hate those words? If outward skin-deep appearance does not equal real beauty, then frumpiness and dowdiness do not equal true spirituality, either.

I am amazed at what products are advertised to make a person sexy. That also seems to sell. I actually have a small hair spray bottle that says, "Happy Birthday, Sexy." I have no idea where it came from. I think it came in the mail. I was at a large department store yesterday looking for some hair spray, and guess what I saw in a big red can? You guessed it, Big Sexy Hair Spray. They also have shampoo and conditioner. Give me a break! If you believe that any particular hair spray will make you sexy, I have a bridge in Brooklyn I want to sell you. Real beauty is more than we can buy in a bottle or a can. But, again, why do we want to be beautiful in the first place? Why do we want to be sexy?

## Our Basic Needs to Be Loved and Significant

I believe we want to be beautiful and sexy because we want to be loved and accepted. But if we believe that it is our outward packaging that will give us love, we will be disappointed. We need to know that these desires to be loved and significant are not just selfish drives. Psychologists tell us that after the basic needs for shelter and food are met, human beings have two driving internal needs: to be loved and to be significant. We may call them by different names—loved, secure, wanted, accepted, or belonging. We might also want to be significant, respected, or capable, which may include the desire for accomplishment and adventure. I believe people have two needs, whatever you want to call them.

The first list seems to be stronger drives in women, and the second for men. The Bible commands men to *"love your wives, just as Christ also loved the church and gave Himself for her"* (Eph. 5:25). The Bible never commands wives to love their husbands; they are commanded to respect and honor their husbands. Interesting how that is. The Bible never scolds women for needing to be loved or tells men to be ashamed of the desire or need to be respected and honored.

It is important that we recognize these as God-given drives or needs. We do not need to be ashamed or embarrassed about them. The question becomes this: How do we righteously fulfill these drives? The drive to belong is very powerful in the teenage years. Teenagers will sometimes do things they do not even want to do in order to be accepted. Guys will engage in risky and dangerous stunts and pursuits to belong and to impress others. Girls will give what they don't want to give away before they want to give it in order to be loved.

We need to teach our kids and young people about these drives. Verbalizing these facts is extremely helpful. These drives are normal. They are God-given. People do not need to be embarrassed or ashamed to want love, acceptance, and significance.

But they need to be careful how they pursue the fulfillment of these needs. Just having this awareness is beneficial to them and to us. The saddest thing that can happen is that we sometimes give up on our dreams for fulfillment. We kill the desires within ourselves. We begin to believe our present lives are as good as it's going to get. We become cynical, jaded, pessimistic, and bored with life. That is not God's answer to dealing with these needs.

Do we make every effort to communicate to our young people that they are loved and significant to us? Donnie came to know he had significance because he was asked to do a very important task, and his dad believed he could do it. His contribution was needed for the operation and success of the farm. His dad believed in him. That is so powerful!

How powerful it would be if every young man had a job to do that was a significant and needed contribution to the family. Girls need to know they are loved unconditionally, that they have great value, and that they have an important role in the family. Parents and families are an important component in giving each child a sense of being loved and valued. I believe this is also a significant task for a loving, family-oriented church and community of believers. That is what the Lord calls His church—a loving, caring, accepting, and nonjudgmental family. But ultimately, these needs in our lives are a vacuum inside of us that only God through the Lord Jesus Christ can fill.

## The Power of What We Believe about Ourselves

When I was a young Christian struggling to be the wife and mother I wanted to be, I would often become discouraged and hard on myself. At those times, my dear friend Juanita would quote Song of Solomon 4:7: *"You are all fair, my love. And there is no spot in you."* That is what the prince said to his beloved. We had studied that passage together, and I knew this was what God was speaking to me. I was seeing all my failures, but Jesus was seeing me as I was in Him.

That verse impacted me every time she quoted it to me. It is so powerful, so motivating to know that the God of all creation believes in us. We speak of the importance of our faith in Jesus—and rightly so—but we need to see that He believes in us. He has faith in us. He knows who we are in Him. He knows what we can become. We must believe what He says of us. Believe Him—not the liar, the accuser of the brethren (and sisters) who says we are trash and failures.

We often believe what others believe about us. And what we believe about ourselves, we often become. We need to visualize success and accomplishment for ourselves and for each other. I am so thankful for my friend Juanita who believed in me and was used of God to remind me that He believed in me.

I had just graduated from the University of Oregon and was starting my first year teaching high school English when I went back to see my high school English teacher from my senior year. I wanted some of the materials she had used. She was married to a local lawyer, and they were considered one of the more prominent families in our little town of Lebanon. My family and I were more or less the invisible citizens overlooked by the affluent. I thanked her for the materials, and as I was leaving, she said almost offhandedly, "You will make a good teacher." Wow! Mrs. Wilshire said I would make a good teacher! That was 55 years ago, but I have never forgotten her comment. I repeat, we often believe what others believe about us. And what we believe about ourselves, we become.

We make a hypothesis about ourselves, and then our brain finds information and confirmation to verify that argument. We decide we are stupid, and then we notice all the dumb things we say or do. We decide we are smart and then notice the smart comments we make or wise things we do. That is similar to buying a car and then noticing that same car all over the highways (we had never noticed them before).

What hypotheses have you made about yourself? Whatever those beliefs are, whether positive or negative, you will find abundant evidence to confirm them. We must reject the statements about ourselves that do not line up with what the word of God says is true. These negative beliefs may come from others, from Satan, or from our own minds, but if they do not agree with Scripture and what Jesus says, then they are not true. That is vitally important. It cannot be overemphasized.

Again, I ask, what are you saying about yourself and to yourself? Listen to your self-talk. Only you can change it. You *must* list positive affirmations about yourself based on the truths of Scripture. Rehearse them, speak them—preferably out loud—even if it feels uncomfortable. It can feel awkward, but speak truth until you feel it and believe it.

Here are some facts about you if you are a born-again believer in the Lord Jesus Christ. These truths give great assurance of significance, acceptance, and security. Believe the word instead of the lies of the enemy.

**In Christ**

These verses give **significance** in Christ

| | |
|---|---|
| *I am the salt and light of the earth* | Matthew 5:13 |
| *I can do all things through Christ who strengthens me* | Philippians 4:13 |
| *I am a branch of the true vine, a channel of His life* | John 15:1, 5 |
| *I am chosen and appointed to bear fruit* | John 15:16 |
| *I may approach God with freedom and confidence* | Ephesians 3:12 |
| *I am God's temple* | 1 Corinthians 3:16 |
| *I am God's workmanship, His masterpiece* | Ephesians 2:10 |
| *I am established, anointed, and sealed by God* | 2 Corinthians 1:21 |
| *I am a new creation in Christ* | 2 Corinthians 5:17 |
| *I am a minister of reconciliation* | 2 Corinthians 5:20 |
| *I am a coworker with God* | 2 Corinthians 6:1 |

These verses give **security and acceptance** in Christ

| | |
|---|---|
| *I am loved and cannot be separated from His love* | Romans 8:35–39 |
| *I am free from condemnation* | Romans 8:1–2 |
| *I am God's child* | John 1:12 |
| *I am Christ's friend* | John 15:15 |
| *I am redeemed and forgiven of all my sins* | Colossians 1:14 |
| *I am complete in Christ* | Colossians 2:10 |
| *I am promised that all things work together for good* | Romans 8:28 |
| *I am confident God will complete His good work in me* | Philippians 1:6 |
| *I am born of God, and the evil one cannot touch me* | 1 John 5:18 |
| *I am a member of Christ's body* | 1 Corinthians 12:27 |
| *I am a citizen of heaven* | Philippians 3:20[1] |

Why? Because God wants it that way *"according to the good pleasure of His will"* (Eph. 1:5). By His grace, I am what He declares me to be. To claim these truths and so many others we find in God's word is not pride; it is faith—a faith that pleases God and without which we cannot please Him. Believe, rehearse, and obey every word in these Scriptural affirmations of your true identity in Christ.

## Chapter Twenty-Five
## Fear of the Lord

The Scriptures contain numerous references to those who fear the Lord.

- *"The secret of the LORD is with those who fear Him"* (Ps. 25:14).
- *"Behold, the eye of the LORD is on those who fear Him, on those who hope in His mercy, to deliver their soul from death, and to keep them alive in famine"* (Ps. 33:18–19).
- *"The angel of the LORD encamps all around those who fear Him, and delivers them"* (Ps. 34:7).
- *"Oh, fear the LORD, you His saints! There is no want to those who fear Him"* (Ps. 34:9).
- *"For as the heavens are high above the earth, so great is His mercy toward those who fear Him"* (Ps. 103:11).
- *"As a father pities his children, so the Lord pities those who fear Him, for He knows our frame; he remembers that we are dust"* (Ps. 103:13–14).
- *"But the mercy of the Lord is from everlasting to everlasting on those who fear Him, and His righteousness to children's children, to such as keep His covenant, and to those who remember His commandments to do them"* (Ps. 103:17–18).
- *"Blessed is the man who fears the Lord, who delights greatly in His commandments. His descendants will be mighty on earth;*

*the generation of the upright will be blessed. Wealth and riches will be in his house, and his righteousness endures forever"* (Ps. 112:1–3).
- *"In the fear of the LORD there is strong confidence, and His children will have a place of refuge"* (Prov. 14:26).
- *"The fear of the LORD is a fountain of life, to turn one away from the snares of death"* (Prov. 14:27).
- *"The fear of the LORD prolongs days, but the years of the wicked will be shortened"* (Prov. 10:27).
- *"The fear of the LORD is the instruction of wisdom, and before honor is humility"* (Prov. 15:33).

## What Is the Fear of the Lord?

Many can quote this Scripture: *"The fear of the LORD is the beginning of wisdom"* (Prov. 9:10). And some can quote this verse: *"Behold, the fear of the Lord, that is wisdom, and to depart from evil is understanding"* (Job 28:28). Deuteronomy 10:12 tells us that fear of the Lord is something God requires of us.

But what is fear of the Lord? Does it mean we are to be afraid of the Lord? Some say it means to respect Him like we respect our fathers and don't want to disobey. Perhaps that comes closer to the truth, but I think there is more.

Deuteronomy 31:12–13 gives further insight. *"Gather the people together . . . that they may hear and that they may learn to fear the LORD your God and carefully observe all the words of this law, and that their children, who have not known it, may hear and learn to fear the LORD your God as long as you live in the land which you cross the Jordan to possess."* Hearing the word must be involved in learning the fear of the Lord.

Psalm 34:11 says, *"Come, you children, listen to me; I will teach you the fear of the LORD."* That suggests it is something we do not know automatically but must learn.

## Fear of the Lord

Psalm 34:15–16 has this secret: *"The eyes of the Lord are on the righteous, and His ears are open to their cry. The face of the LORD is against those who do evil, to cut off the remembrance of them from the earth."*

That, my dear hearts, is the fear of the Lord—knowing that He is present with us, and that His eyes are always on us, and that He always hears us when we cry out to Him. That is what it means to fear the Lord. He is with us. He sees us. He hears our cries. We get so busy and distracted that we sometimes forget this.

I remember the time when Donnie was choking on meat. After several minutes of trying in all the wrong ways to help him and realizing he was about to pass out, I cried out, "Oh, Jesus, help us." As I did, Donnie said the meat was gone, and he could breathe.

But it takes practice to learn the skill of walking moment by moment in the awareness of God's presence. I was new at this practice, and it took me several minutes of thinking of every possible source of help before realizing no help was available and I would have to cry out to Jesus. I think learning to trust an invisible God is like teaching children they have an imaginary friend who is always with them—except God is not imaginary.

Of course, the fear of the Lord is also recognizing that He will ultimately turn His face against evildoers (verse 16). He is a righteous God who will bring about His holy justice.

## Chapter Twenty-Six
## Beauty for Ashes

The Bible actually has a great deal to say about beauty. Peter speaks of the *"incorruptible beauty of a gentle and quiet spirit, which is very precious in the sight of God"* (1 Pet. 3:4). This *"hidden person of the heart"* (1 Pet. 3:4) is more important than the outward adornment of *"arranging the hair, wearing gold, or putting on fine apparel"* (1 Pet. 3:3). That suggests a beauty of character. It doesn't mean we shouldn't wear jewelry, and it doesn't mean we shouldn't arrange our hair or wear clothes. That clearly wasn't Peter's or God's intention.

Since Peter tells us that this beauty pleases the Lord, a thorough study of this passage is abundantly profitable. Developing godly character and qualities of kindness, joy, patience, and gentleness is of the utmost importance. The Bible speaks of the beauty of holiness. Incidentally, Proverbs tells us that a nagging, complaining wife is like a dripping faucet. Picture that. Not a pretty sight!

A beautiful woman knows who she is. She accepts the way she looks, feels, and thinks and does not try to change herself to look like someone else. She is open and honest, unafraid to share what is going on inside with people she trusts. She is loving, forgiving, and accepting of others because she knows she is loved, forgiven, and accepted. She has come to trust who she is, who God made her to be, warts and all.

Because of the cleansing blood of the Lord Jesus Christ, she does not hide or walk in shame or fear. She knows she is a flawed human being living in a broken, fallen, damaged world, but she is *"accepted in the Beloved"* (Eph. 1:6). She is courageous enough to be honest about her weaknesses *and* her strengths. She is full of the beauty that flows from her capacity to see the beauty all around her in others and in the world God has created. She is full of beauty because she sees beauty. A young Christian man from Bosnia told me he had not seen the colors and beauty all around him in flowers, trees, and nature until he became a believer. A beautiful woman is full of the beauty God has placed in her.

Elizabeth Barrett Browning wrote in her poem "Aurora Leigh":

Earth's crammed with heaven,
And every common bush afire with God;
But only he who sees, takes off his shoes,
The rest sit round it and pluck blackberries.[1] [or look at their smartphones?]

We are told of Abraham's wife Sarah in Genesis 12:14 that *"when Abram came into Egypt, that the Egyptians saw the woman, that she was very beautiful."* It must have been an outward beauty. They saw it. We are also told in the book of Esther that the queen was *"lovely and beautiful"* (Esther 2:7). Esther was given *"six months with oil of myrrh, and six months with perfumes and preparations"* (Esther 2:12). Second Samuel 14:27 points out that David's son Absalom had a daughter named Tamar who was *"a woman of beautiful appearance."* We are seldom told if the beauty being referenced is an outward or an inward beauty, or both.

God recognizes beauty. He grants beauty. I remember walking through the halls of the high school one morning where I taught and noticing that all the young girls were actually beautiful. I told my own girls and the high school girls in my classes that they each had a unique beauty given by God at birth. It was up to them what they would do with it. But I warned them that with age, they would begin to develop their own beauty or lack thereof.

Bitterness, anger, hatred, unkindness, jealousy, envy, meanness, selfishness—all these attitudes and qualities would begin to show up in their faces, especially around the eyes and the mouth. Some of these attitudes can actually kill cells in your body.[2] But with attitudes of love, kindness, patience, forgiveness, and joy, a glow will show up, a glow of beauty from a lifetime lived in love that I believe actually shows up in the face. Some older women are beautiful, and some are just old and haggard.

One of the more interesting references to beautiful women is in Job. After Job's great suffering and loss, we are told that the *"Lord blessed the latter days of Job more than his beginning"* (Job 42:12). God restored Job's wealth to twice what it had been. It says he had ten more children—seven sons and three daughters. *"In all the land were found no women so beautiful as the daughters of Job; and their father gave them an inheritance among their brothers"* (Job 42:15), which was not common in those days. Interestingly, Scripture does not give the names of the sons but does give the names of the three daughters.

The meanings of the names of Job's daughters are most fascinating. The first one he named Jemimah, which is the symbol of a dove and signifies peace and grace. The second one he named Keziah, or Cassia, which refers to fragrance or incense, like the fragrant spices the wise men brought to Jesus—very expensive, rare, and beautiful. The name signified an intrinsic beauty and a testimony that warmth and perfume and fruit had again filled Job's life. The third one he named Keren-Happuch, which means horn of adornment and is a reference to an outward beauty that comes from an inward character. It could suggest cosmetics. Peace, fragrance, and beauty are the fruits of Job's trials.

I rejoice in the victory and triumph I see in my daughters as they have grown through and beyond their battles. They are overcomers; they are victorious. I see restoration and grace that would not have been evident had they not gone through difficult times. There is a kindness, gentleness, understanding, and compassion they have learned in the process. I am proud of their overcoming spirits, knowing the Lord will continue to use these graces in their lives and in the lives of others. Through pain and brokenness, they (and I) have been given the opportunity to be trophies of God's grace. Is this not what our triumph is all about, *to put Christ on display in the way we love others*? I think I comprehend a little of what Job felt when he named his three daughters.

## Chapter Twenty-Seven
## An Eternal Perspective

Is heaven and eternity our focus? Is it our controlling and predominant perspective? Probably not. We are so consumed with the pursuits of this world that heaven is only a distant reality, rarely foremost in our thinking. Our theology teaches that there is a hell to shun and a heaven to gain, but this theology can have little impact or influence on how we live.

Most Christians would say they believe that heaven is real, but they live as though it is irrelevant. Blinded to eternity, the quality of life is measured by the accumulation of stuff and pursuing power and position. We want peace and prosperity—the best of food, drink, pleasure, and possessions—in the here and now. The problem is that the things we pursue and even attain in this world are never as fulfilling as we hoped they would be.

We plan for weeks for a vacation but come home tired and dissatisfied. We save to buy more stuff, but it is never enough. We want more. Anticipated fun and pleasure can be dull, shallow, and unfulfilling. A new car becomes old and out of date. A new house becomes familiar and not so exciting.

When I was so thrilled about building our beautiful home after Bible school, a friend told me the newness and excitement would soon wear off. I remember purposing in my heart to not allow the gratefulness and delight to dissipate. I retained my gratefulness but did become accustomed to the house, and the excitement went away. Fourteen years later, we moved into another new house. The newness and excitement evaporated there, too.

> Without an eternal perspective, we are not equipped to see any redemptive purpose in the pain, and we lose hope and meaning.

Why? Because we are created for something more. It's not that our pursuits and hopes are evil in themselves, but if our driving hopes are based on what the here and now offers, life eventually becomes empty and disappointing. And when stress, pain, and earthly tragedies come, our devastation can turn to despair. Without an eternal perspective, we are not equipped to see any redemptive purpose in the pain, and we lose hope and meaning.

## Finishing Well

I am ending my book with the topic of finishing well because Donnie used to quip that he always read the end of a book first because he wanted to see if it was worth reading. That was a joke, but he was actually referring to the Bible. (I believe he was teaching through Revelation at the time.) And as he said, it ends well. We win!

As Donnie and I approached our 70s, we spoke often about our desire to finish well, to end our lives in a manner well pleasing to the Lord. We knew of a number of highly respected ministers who had fallen away from their service and walk with the Lord in their final years and had not finished well. Scripture also records certain individuals who started well but fell away from faithfully following

God. I think of King Saul, Jehoshaphat, and even King Solomon who, with all his wisdom, didn't finish so well.

Let me assure you, Donnie finished well. Even when the cancer prevented him from standing to preach, there were times when he preached sitting in his wheelchair. He went to be with the Lord in 2009, faithfully serving and magnifying his Savior. And of course, the responsibility of designing his tombstone, our tombstone, fell to me. How do you decide what to say, knowing it will literally be set in stone?

Of course, our names with the year of our births plus the date of his death would be there, but what else of significance should be included? As I recalled our discussion, I thought it appropriate for it to simply say, "He finished well." Since this was a joint tombstone, I told the stonemason to leave space before "He" where a "T" could be placed later, and to leave a space after the "e" where a "y" could be added. When my time comes and someone adds the year of my death, I have told my children to decide if Mom finished well. If so, they can add the "T" and the "y" to make it say *"They* finished well."

Right now, I am still living in the dash between my birth date and the date of my death. Those words written in stone haunt me. I am compelled to finish living my life in a way that honors the Lord. What will the people who know me well think if they only see "HE finished well" on that gravestone? More importantly, what would God think? This stone is a reminder of the need to keep my focus on eternity.

This perspective influences many of my daily decisions. Psalm 90:12 spoke to me many years ago concerning the brevity of life: *"So teach us to number our days, that we may gain a heart of wisdom."* Without the realization that our days are limited, we have not even begun to gain wisdom. Psalm 31:15 says, *"My times are in Your hand."* God knows our days, but we do not. We need to live according to His wisdom as revealed in Scripture. The saddest thing is when people have no purpose to sustain them in their waning years of life.

Another Scripture that encourages me to finish well is 1 Thessalonians 5:23: *"Now may the God of peace Himself sanctify you completely; and may your whole spirit, soul, and body be preserved blameless at the coming of our Lord Jesus Christ."* But the most reassuring verse of all is the next one, verse 24: *"He who calls you is faithful, who also will do it."*

It is *"the God of peace Himself"* who sanctifies. I intend with Christ's help to finish well because my God is faithful, and He will do it. *Oh Lord, keep me focused on You and eternity.*

# Notes

### Chapter Seventeen: What I Have Learned
1. William Shakespeare, *As You Like It*, Act II, Scene VII, http://shakespeare.mit.edu/asyoulikeit/full.html.
2. William Shakespeare, *Macbeth*, Act V, Scene V, http://shakespeare.mit.edu/macbeth/full.html.
3. Ibid.
4. Westminster Shorter Catechism, *Fisher's Catechism*, https://reformed.org/documents/wsc/index.html?_top=https://reformed.org/documents/WSC.html.

### Chapter Eighteen: Let's Learn from Job
1. *Forrest Gump*, http://www.imsdb.com/scripts/Forrest-Gump.html.

### Chapter Nineteen: Do Not Give Up Your Dreams
1. Corinne J. Naden and Rose Blue, *Wilma Rudolph (African-American Biographies)* (Chicago: Raintree, 2004), 7.
2. Byline by George Herman ("Babe") Ruth in "Bat It Out!" *The Rotarian*, 1940.

### Chapter Twenty-Two: Choices We Must Make
1. Amy Carmichael, "In Acceptance Lieth Peace," *New Things*, https://newthingspringingforth.wordpress.com/2013/05/07/in-acceptance-lieth-peace/.

2. Reinhold Neibuhr, "Serenity Prayer," http://www.beliefnet.com/prayers/protestant/addiction/serenity-prayer.aspx.
3. Johnson Oatman, "Count Your Blessings," *Hymnary.org*, https://hymnary.org/text/when_upon_lifes_billows_you_are_tempest.

## Chapter Twenty-Three: Right Thinking about Pleasure
1. "The Declaration of Independence," http://www.ushistory.org/declaration/document/.
2. George Bernard Shaw, *Man and Superman, Act IV*. https://ebooks.adelaide.edu.au/s/shaw/george_bernard/man_and_superman/act4.html.

## Chapter Twenty-Four: Finding Joy and Beauty in Serving Others
1. Taken from: THE BONDAGE BREAKER: registered: Copyright: copyright: 1990, 1993, 2000 by Neil T. Anderson Published by Harvest House Publishers Eugene, Oregon 97408 www.harvesthousepublishers.com Used by Permission.

## Chapter Twenty-Six: Beauty for Ashes
1. Elizabeth Barrett Browning, "Aurora Leigh," Seventh Book, 1864, http://digital.library.upenn.edu/women/barrett/aurora/aurora.html.
2. Ruth Buczynski, Ph.D., "How Anger Affects the Brain and Body," National Institute for the Clinical Application of Behavioral Medicine, http://www.nicabm.com/how-anger-affects-the-brain-and-body-infographic/.

## About the Author

Carol Bayne (www.carolbayne.com) is a blogger, author, and speaker. Her husband, Don Bayne, pastored Grace Bible Fellowship for 33 years until his death in 2009, and Carol served the church as Women's Ministries Director. She is the mother of four, grandmother of nine, and great-grandmother of one. She graduated from University of Oregon with a bachelor's degree plus a fifth year majoring in English and education. She taught high school English a number of years and taught two years at Prairie Bible Institute in Alberta, Canada. She is currently married to Arthur Mueller.

CPSIA information can be obtained
at www.ICGtesting.com
Printed in the USA
BVHW071102261118
534009BV00006B/573/P

9 781632 963079